Praise For **America's First**

*I had never even heard of John Ro~~lfe~~ ~~before~~ ~~being~~
introduced to a delightful book about his life in early
America. This book is another testament to the amazing
power of influence. One person can indeed change the
whole world.* – Dave Johnson, Nikken Royal
Ambassador

*John Rolfe is the origin story of the American Free
Enterprise system. I'm inspired all over again by John L.
Rolfe's presentation.* – Reid Nelson, Network Marketing
Entrepreneur

*Wow, this was a fascinating journey, a very exciting
story with great insights for budding entrepreneurs. I
was intrigued with the real story of John Rolfe and
Pocahontas. I had no real idea of the trials and
tribulations of the time.* – John David Rolfe, serial
entrepreneur

Absolutely loved the story! Inspiring. – Albert A.
Mazzone, serial entrepreneur and CEO Horn and Hardart
Brands

*The ultimate risk/reward quest in starting a new
business! John Rolfe showed great marketing skills and
political acumen in both the new and old world, and
these are a must if one wants to become a serious
entrepreneur. A great read of both history and how and
what is needed to succeed in the business world.* – Lee
Stivale, retired corporate executive

His perseverance was amazing! As a history buff, I was amazed what I learned about early settlement in Virginia. – H.L. Chalfant, antiques dealer and history buff

AMERICA'S FIRST ENTREPRENEUR

HOW JOHN ROLFE'S COURAGE, PERSISTENCE, AND RELATIONSHIPS CHANGED THE WORLD

JOHN L. ROLFE

Ambassador Family Press
West Chester, PA

AMERICA'S FIRST ENTREPRENEUR

ISBN-13: 978-1467950817
ISBN-10: 1467950815

Ambassador Family Press
West Chester, PA

TABLE OF CONTENTS

AMERICA'S FIRST ENTREPRENEUR

HOW JOHN ROLFE'S COURAGE, PERSISTENCE, AND RELATIONSHIPS CHANGED THE WORLD

JOHN L. ROLFE

PREFACE

What is being an entrepreneur all about? The dictionary defines an entrepreneur as "a person who organizes and manages any enterprise, especially a business, usually with considerable initiative and risk."

Who becomes an entrepreneur, and why would you want to be an entrepreneur? Here it is in four words. Creation. Freedom. Money. Legacy.

Being an entrepreneur is all about creating a venture that you have some control over, achieving the freedom to live life as you wish – doing what you want, when you want, where you want, and how you want – acquiring the money or wealth to do so, and leaving a business or financial legacy. And, oh, enjoying the game along the way.

Why do you need this book? This book will give you time-tested principles of entrepreneurship which will help you succeed in reaching your goals. America's first entrepreneur illustrates all the important principles of entrepreneurship. America's first entrepreneur was wildly successful within seven years using these principles after a series of seemingly insurmountable obstacles. His epic story is very inspiring. The industry America's first entrepreneur created is not only still successful in America after 400 years, but has multi-billion dollar sales year in and year out.

I'm sure you've already read all the dire statistics about how the odds are stacked against you in starting a business and how few new businesses succeed. Yet you are right to have confidence that your business will beat the odds and succeed. Without that belief you and your business will fail.

This book will help you avoid the mistakes that may not be obvious to many of the entrepreneurs who start businesses. I certainly hope your challenges won't be nearly as tough as those actually faced and overcome by America's first entrepreneur. But the dramatic events of his life graphically illustrate the kinds of challenges every entrepreneur faces. And it's a great story even if you're not an entrepreneur.

In each chapter you will find the inspiring true and epic story of the challenges faced by America's first entrepreneur. As you enjoy the historical narrative, think about your own entrepreneurial venture and consider whether you have met your similar business challenges. It was an amazing time in history, and the end of each chapter highlights some key events going on elsewhere in the world at the same time.

Once you have absorbed the wisdom presented by the story of America's first entrepreneur, you can be sure your belief that your business is going to succeed is rooted in sound entrepreneurial principles, not in la-la land like your relatives probably think and say.

Because I was named for the historical John Rolfe, I've heard about John Rolfe and Pocahontas my entire life. I didn't appreciate his critical role in the success of England colonizing America until a visit to Jamestown, Virginia, set me on a path of serious research into the life of John Rolfe. By a happy coincidence, I was already researching entrepreneurship. I discovered that John Rolfe was America's first entrepreneur and he set the tone for the unique American spirit of entrepreneurship.

As you will see, without John Rolfe's two major contributions, the Virginia colony would have failed and the French, Spanish, and Dutch, rather than the English, would have colonized not only New Mexico, California, Florida, Canada, Delaware, and New York, but most of what is now the United States. In a very real sense, John Rolfe is responsible for the United States being an English speaking nation.

Jamestown was the first permanent English settlement in the Americas, thirteen years before the Virginia Company of London granted a land patent to colonists on the *Mayflower* allowing them to settle at the mouth of the Hudson River in 1620. However, they sailed to the north and settled in what is now New England.

The Virginia colony was in serious trouble financially and the colonists were constantly dwindling in number and strength because of disease, starvation, and Indian attacks, and likely wouldn't survive. Two accomplishments by John Rolfe turned things around for Jamestown, for Virginia, and ultimately for the future United States.

John Rolfe's first contribution was his sole responsibility for the economic success of the Virginia colony. For years the colony could find no gold, silver, pearls, or cash crop. John Rolfe developed the first and only cash crop, which assured the success of the colony and made it not only viable but wildly successful financially. The History Channel's 2010 production ***America: The Story of Us*** called Jamestown after the success of John Rolfe's tobacco America's first boomtown. Without the entrepreneurship of John Rolfe, Jamestown would have been a ghost town.

Second, John Rolfe fell in love with Princess Pocahontas. He asked for and received permission from the Governor of Virginia to marry Pocahontas, recognizing that interracial marriage was at least discouraged if not prohibited. No white man had ever married a Native American. He also asked for and received permission from Pocahontas' father, Chief Powhatan, the paramount chief of 31 Algonquin tribes. John Rolfe and Princess Pocahontas were married on April 5, 1614.

Notably, the wedding of John Rolfe and Pocahontas was the first interracial church marriage in the New World. John Rolfe's initiative in his personal life as well as his business life set an enduring precedent for American life.

Pocahontas' marriage to Rolfe led to a period of peace, known as The Peace of Pocahontas, which allowed the English foothold in Jamestown to expand until there were too many English for the natives to kill or expel. This period of peace was directly responsible for the success of the Virginia colony, and John Rolfe was responsible for it.

John Rolfe's two important contributions, the financial success and the period of peace for the first permanent English colony in the Americas, led to the establishment of the English common law and the English cultural heritage of representative government and religious freedom on which the United States of America was founded. If John Rolfe hadn't created a financially successful industry and fallen in love with Pocahontas, we could have a French, Spanish, or even Dutch heritage.

But before he could accomplish all this, as you will soon see, John Rolfe's entrepreneurial challenges included an Atlantic crossing on the *Sea Venture* that was so extraordinary that it became the inspiration for William Shakespeare's play *The Tempest*.

John L. Rolfe

Chapter 1

THE THREE G'S: GOLD, GLORY, AND GOD

SEEING POSSIBILITIES

As John Rolfe boards the *Sea Venture* in London, England on May 15, 1609, for his epic adventure, who would have thought that he, John Rolfe, a 24 year old gentleman farmer, would in a period of only seven years assure the success of English colonial efforts in America, marry the most important woman in Colonial America, succeed as America's first entrepreneur becoming the father of American capitalism, create America's largest export for the next 150 years, and create a billion dollar industry that still thrives after 400 years. In addition, who would have thought he would become a member of the first representative legislative body in the Americas, a fundamental institution that would lead to our uniquely American form of government. Certainly not John Rolfe, and most certainly not anyone else.

SEEKING HIS FORTUNE ACROSS THE SEA IN VIRGINIA

The *Sea Venture* is the flagship of the nine vessel fleet assembled to rescue the so-far disastrous two year old attempt to establish an English colony in Jamestown, Virginia. John Rolfe had his 24th birthday just nine days before, on May 6, 1609. He is a gentleman farmer, not an adventurer, soldier, or craftsman like most of the passengers. And to underscore the fact he is a settler not an adventurer, he is accompanied by his wife, Sarah Hacker, whom he married the previous year. Although she probably doesn't realize it yet, Sarah is likely pregnant with their first child when she boards the *Sea Venture*.

JOHN ROLFE'S FAMILY HISTORY

John Rolfe and a twin brother Eustacius were born and baptized in the parish church in the village of Heacham, county of Norfolk, England, about 110 miles north of London, on May 3, 1585, during the reign of Queen Elizabeth I. This was three years before the English navy under Sir Francis Drake defeated the Spanish Armada on August 8, 1588, and thus became the most powerful European nation. John's twin brother Eustacius died 27 days after his birth, on June 2, 1585. If you noticed that May 3, 1585, is different than the usually quoted date of May 6, the Norfolk Record Office, county of Norfolk, England, issued a correction in 2012, after reviewing the Heacham village church records in its possession.

John Rolfe is named for his father John Rolfe. His father was born October 17, 1562. John Rolfe's mother was Dorothea or Dorothy Mason, born in 1559. John Rolfe the father died when John Rolfe was eight years old, on November 29, 1593. John Rolfe's grandfather died the same year. His mother Dorothy remarried on March 9, 1594, to Robert Redman. So we can assume John Rolfe's childhood was difficult.

ENJOYING A PIPE

As a young adult, John Rolfe likes to smoke a pipe of tobacco. A gentleman typically smokes only one bowl of a pipe in an evening. So the quantity of tobacco smoked is nothing like the quantity of cigarettes, which were developed 200 years later, smoked by a typical smoker today.

In Rolfe's time clay pipes for smoking tobacco are very small. The tiny bowl of the pipe holds only about one twenty-fifth of an ounce of tobacco. You can see an historic pipe in the museum at Jamestown. The entire bowl of the clay pipe is about the size of the tip of my little finger from the bottom of the fingernail to the end, and I have small hands.

In the early 1600's, tobacco wasn't the demon that many of us see it as today. In the late 1500's and early 1600's, tobacco was used both by the Virginia Indians and by the English for medicinal purposes. The Indians also used it for ceremonial purposes.

Tobacco is introduced into England in 1556 by a sailor, and it is a mild tobacco from the Spanish controlled Caribbean. Tobacco becomes popular in England for recreational purposes sometime between 1565 and 1590. On June 18, 1586, Francis Drake takes the remaining settlers from Roanoke Island back to England, arriving on July 28, 1586. They bring with them tobacco pipes, tobacco seeds, and tobacco plants.

In the early 1600's, all farming is organic. Chemical pesticides, herbicides, and fertilizers would not be developed for centuries. And mineral fertilizers were not used, unlike today when mineral fertilizers are mined from areas high in radon. Thus, there were no toxic chemicals emanating from the tobacco smoke. Also, tobacco hadn't yet been bred to maximize the concentration of nicotine. So tobacco didn't have all the disadvantages it has today.

Tobacco smoking did produce smoke, which could be annoying to others, as King James I noted in his diatribe against tobacco. And it could be bad for one's lungs, although in the London air thick with coal smoke, one might hardly notice.

FINDING A MARKET NEED

John Rolfe sees an opportunity, he identifies a market need that people will pay for, to break the Spanish monopoly of the mild tobacco the English prefer. Rolfe's goal in traveling to Virginia is to grow the mild Spanish tobacco in Virginia, cure it, and export it to England at great profit, thereby bettering himself.

Rolfe takes care of the money or investment needed for every entrepreneurial venture by buying shares in the Virginia Company of London. He thereby secures passage to Virginia for himself and his wife, and land for planting in Virginia.

THE THREE G'S

The Virginia Company of London proclaims that Protestant English colonization of America is God's will. They get ministers to preach that God wants a Protestant English colony in Virginia rather than a Catholic Spanish colony like Mexico, most of South America and Central America, and St. Augustine in what is now Florida. The Virginia Company of London also preaches that it is God's will to evangelize and convert the native savages of Virginia to the Protestant religion. So Rolfe's goals are in line with what today are called the three G's of colonization, Gold (literally or figuratively), Glory (of self and/or King and country), and God.

TOBACCO SEEDS

Rolfe is almost certainly carrying some of the difficult to obtain seeds of Spanish tobacco with him on the *Sea Venture*. Tobacco seeds are very tiny, so it would be easy to carry a large quantity of them, and many historians believe he did carry them. The seeds are difficult to obtain because the Spanish have a monopoly on the mild sweet tobacco (a much harsher variety is native to Virginia) and forbid anyone to sell tobacco seeds to a non-Spaniard under penalty of death.

Since these tobacco seeds of Caribbean tobacco were central to John Rolfe's entrepreneurial vision and plan, I can't imagine he would have left everything he knew and travelled to Virginia with his wife unless he had a supply of tobacco seeds with him.

THE LONG OCEAN VOYAGE TO VIRGINIA

On May 5, 1609, the Virginia Company of London sends Captain Samuel Argall to Virginia to explore a more direct route to Virginia instead of going south along the coasts of Europe and Africa and then sailing west to the Caribbean and then north up the Gulf Stream along the Atlantic coast of America. The traditional southern route is the one John Rolfe and the *Sea Venture* will take ten days later.

The rationale for trying a more northern route is twofold. First, despite the peace treaty of 1604 between England and Spain, the Spanish are attacking English ships in the Caribbean. For example, in 1606, the *Richard*, a ship of the Virginia Company of Plymouth which holds the royal charter for more northern lands, sails the traditional route to the Americas and is then to head up to Pemaquid on the Maine coast north of the Kennebec River, but it is captured by a Spanish ship and all hands are sent to Spain and imprisoned. The second reason is to see if they can find a faster route to Virginia.

COMING SOON, THE THIRD SUPPLY

Captain Samuel Argall, who looms large later in the history of Jamestown, reaches Jamestown on July 13, 1609, in only nine weeks instead of the usual 16 weeks. But the *Sea Venture* fleet doesn't know this, as it departs only ten days after Argall. Captain Argall tells the colonists in Jamestown that the Third Supply fleet will be arriving soon.

ROLFE'S COMMITTED DECISION

John Rolfe is ambitious, brave, and committed to his goal and his enterprise. He has to be, as he is facing a dangerous voyage and dicey conditions in Virginia where so many have already died in the previous two years. Rolfe would have known about the large proportion of deaths among the adventurers from disease and Indian attack, as returning ships told the news. Rolfe is also the only person going to Virginia with the intent to grow tobacco and make it into a profitable export crop.

SHIPBOARD ACCOMODATIONS

Rolfe is facing what is expected to be a 16 week journey aboard a crowded, sailing ship. At about 100 feet long overall from the bowsprit to the aft of the main deck, or slightly less than the length of six Chrysler 300 sedans, the *Sea Venture* is the largest ship in the fleet. It carries 153 people, 118 passengers and 35 crew, plus supplies for 16 weeks of sailing and for many months of living in Virginia. Of course, there is no dining room, no bathroom, and no entertainment. It is nothing like a modern cruise ship. There is little to do, and passengers usually have to stay below deck so the sailors have room for their sailing duties.

SQUARE RIGGED

Sailing ships in 1609 do not have engines or motors, oars, or GPS. They are entirely at the mercy of the wind, waves, and tides. The ships sailing in the Atlantic are square rigged rather than triangular lateen rigged as is often the case in the Mediterranean Sea. Square rigged sails do very well when the wind is behind the ship. Because the Atlantic Ocean had steady wind patterns, this was an advantage. Triangular lateen rigged ships are more maneuverable but much slower when there is a steady wind behind the ship.

THE GULF STREAM AND OTHER OCEAN CURRENTS AND WINDS

You've heard of the Gulf Stream I'm sure. It's a warm current that flows from the Caribbean north along the eastern seaboard of the United States and then turns east across the North Atlantic Ocean to England. The clockwise rotation of the current continues south along the west coast of Europe and North Africa, and then turns west across the Atlantic towards the Caribbean to complete a circle of the Atlantic Ocean north of the equator. The prevailing winds follow the current and rotate clockwise as well.

In good weather, the journey from England to Virginia takes approximately 16 weeks, or four months, almost one-third of a year, going with the currents and prevailing winds. The journey is uncomfortable at best.

JOHN ROLFE AND SARAH ROLFE SAIL ON THE SAME SHIP, UNLIKE OTHER COUPLES, AND INTEND TO SETTLE IN VIRGINIA

Rolfe's ambition, bravery, and commitment all show in his decision to bring his wife along with him. Most of the men consider themselves adventurers, not settlers, and leave their wives in England. Since Sarah Rolfe is recently pregnant, she would be especially uncomfortable on the journey. Sarah Rolfe is, perhaps, even braver than John Rolfe, as she is one of very few women to go to Virginia.

John Rolfe is fortunate that his wife accompanies him on the same ship, the *Sea Venture*. Edward Eason and his wife also sail together on the *Sea Venture*. But several other adventures on the *Sea Venture*, William Pierce and Captain George Yeardley, bring their wives along to Virginia, but their wives sail on different ships. William Pierce's wife Joan and his 10-year-old daughter Jane sail on the *Blessing*. Some years later, the daughter Jane Pierce will become very important to John Rolfe. Captain Yeardley's wife Temperance sails on the *Falcon*.

Perhaps having his wife with him on the flagship of the fleet is an indication of John Rolfe's people skills which would later show themselves in his political and marketing astuteness.

SAILING ABOARD THE FLAGSHIP, THE *SEA VENTURE*

On May 15, 1609, John Rolfe and his wife Sarah board the *Sea Venture*. After all have boarded the *Sea Venture* and six other ships at the wharf in London's Woolwich docks, the seven ships sail down the Thames River toward the English Channel. It takes several days. Then the ships sail west along the English Channel to the port of Plymouth to meet the other two ships, the small pinnace *Virginia* and the even smaller unnamed ketch, to bring the fleet to a total of nine ships.

The flagship, admiral, and largest ship in the fleet is the *Sea Venture*, commanded by Captain Christopher Newport. Newport also captained the *Susan Constant*, the flagship of the first fleet of three ships to arrive in Jamestown in 1607. He also captained the First Supply and the Second Supply. This, the Third Supply, is Captain Newport's fourth crossing to Virginia. Other leaders on board are the Admiral of the fleet and fleet commander, Sir George Somers, and the new Governor of Virginia, General Sir Thomas Gates.

OTHER PASSENGERS OF NOTE ON THE *SEA VENTURE*

Two Indians, Namontack and Matchumps, who earlier were sent to England by John Smith, are returning to Virginia. Reverend Richard Bucke, an Anglican minister, age 27, is on board. Also on board are Captain George Yeardley whose wife Temperance sails on the *Falcon*; William Pierce whose wife Joan and 10 year old daughter Jane sail on the *Blessing*; Mistress Horton and her maid Elizabeth Persons; William Strachey, the gentleman poet who knows Ben Jonson and other literary types and who will become Secretary of the colony and who writes a detailed account of his adventures; Ralph Hamor, who will become Secretary of the colony after Strachey; Stephen Hopkins, a preachy Puritan layman who will later go to the Plymouth Colony with his wife and children but who leaves them behind in England for his Virginia adventure; and Silvester Jourdain, who writes an account of his adventures.

THE OTHER SHIPS OF THE FLEET

The second largest ship of the fleet is the *Diamond*. It is the vice admiral and is commanded by Captain John Ratcliffe who was captain of the *Discovery*, one of the three ships that arrived in Jamestown in 1607. The *Falcon* is the rear admiral or third largest ship of the fleet. It is commanded by Captain John Martin, one of the original Virginia settlers who returned to England in 1608 and is on his way back to Jamestown. The *Falcon*'s sailing master is Francis Nelson, who went to Jamestown in 1608 as captain of the *Phoenix*, a pinnace that took 40 settlers to Jamestown as part of the First Supply.

The fourth ship in the fleet is the *Blessing* captained by Gabriel Archer. The fifth ship is the *Unity*. The sixth ship is the *Lion*. The seventh ship of the fleet is the *Swallow*. On the *Swallow* as sailing master is the nephew of Admiral George Somers, Matthew Somers. The eighth ship is the pinnace *Virginia* which was the first ship built in North America in the failed Popham colony at Sagadahoc, Maine. It is commanded by Captain James Davies who was on the expedition to Maine. The ninth ship is a small unnamed ketch.

LOADING MORE PROVISIONS IN PLYMOUTH, ENGLAND

On May 20, 1609, the fleet arrives in Plymouth on the southern coast of England, a port protected by the Isle of Wight. It has taken five days to sail down the Thames River to the English Channel, then south and west along the Channel to Plymouth. In Plymouth the fleet of seven ships from London meets up with its other two members so that all nine ships are together. Now the final provisions are put on board. The main food supplies are hogsheads, or large casks, of five tons of salt beef, casks of salt pork and salt cod, tons of hard biscuits, beans, oatmeal, flour, butter, cheese, and beer. The water of the time isn't usually clean and pure, so people drink weak beer or some other drink with a little alcohol in it to kill the germs and parasites.

All is in readiness and on the evening of June 2, 1609, the winds and tides are favorable and the fleet sails from Plymouth.

FINALLY, SAILING FROM FALMOUTH, ENGLAND, AND LEAVING ENGLISH WATERS

Shortly after leaving Plymouth, the winds change and the fleet has to put in at Falmouth, farther along the south coast of England. Six days later, on June 8, 1609, the winds are favorable and the fleet sails again.

Because of the distance from London to the south England ports, the loading of final provisions, and the need to wait for favorable winds to sail south along the European coast, the journey has now been more than three weeks and they are just leaving English waters.

SECOND CHARTER OF THE VIRGINIA COMPANY OF LONDON

On May 23, 1609, King James signs the second charter of the Virginia Company of London, updating it. Among other changes, the territory of the Virginia Company of London is now 200 miles north and south of Point Comfort on the Chesapeake Bay.

AVOIDING SPANISH CONTROLLED AREAS

Admiral Somers, General Gates, and Captain Newport decide to try to avoid the Spanish controlled waters and cut across the Atlantic Ocean farther north than usual, but not quite as far north as Captain Samuel Argall is exploring at the same time.

THE *VIRGINIA* TURNS BACK FOR REPAIRS

A week into the voyage the *Virginia* discovers it is leaking seriously and turns back for repairs, so the fleet is reduced to eight ships. The *Virginia* will continue on to Jamestown after repairs.

SMOOTH SAILING FOR SEVEN WEEKS

For seven weeks the voyage is relatively smooth. John and Sarah Rolfe have now been on board for 10 weeks including the time in English coastal waters and English ports.

Sarah Rolfe is probably experiencing morning sickness from her pregnancy. There is little or no privacy. And the food gets worse as they run out of fresh produce. Still, seven weeks of calm seas and good weather is wonderful.

Then the winds come up ….

MEANWHILE, ELSEWHERE, THIS IS HAPPENING …

Quebec City, in New France, founded by Samuel de Champlain on July 3, 1608, has been in existence for over a year now.

Chapter 2

THE TEMPEST

A HURRICANE, CYCLONE, OR TEMPEST

Today the word cyclone is used in the South Pacific for what we usually call a hurricane. In 1609 England, the word is tempest.

After ten weeks on board and seven weeks of smooth sailing on John Rolfe's first ocean crossing, he experiences the storm of the century, the worst tempest that any of the seasoned voyagers on the *Sea Venture* have ever seen.

WILLIAM STRACHEY'S ACCOUNT OF THE TEMPEST

William Strachey, who was aboard the *Sea Venture* with John Rolfe, was born in 1572 in Essex of minor gentry. He entered Cambridge University in 1588. In 1605 he was in London as a member of Gray's Inn where he studied law. He is a stockholder in Blackfriars Theater and has many friends in literary circles. He is close friends with John Donne, Thomas Campion, and Ben Jonson. He certainly has friends in common with and probably knows William Shakespeare. In 1606 Strachey became secretary to the English ambassador to

Constantinople, Turkey, and moved there. They didn't get along and Strachey was fired. He returned to London in 1608. He buys two shares in the Virginia Company of London, and in 1609 he sails on the *Sea Venture* to Jamestown.

Strachey writes a long letter describing the voyage to Virginia on the *Sea Venture* to a lady in London, thought to be Lady Sara Smythe, wife of Sir Thomas Smythe, Treasurer of the Virginia Company of London and organizer of the details of the expeditions to Virginia. He starts by describing sailing from Plymouth Sound on June 2, 1609, and the ships keeping in sight of each other until St. James Day, Monday, July 24, 1609. He says that Captain Newport reckons they are only seven or eight days from Cape Henry on the Virginia coast at the time. Strachey relates that, starting the night before, Sunday night, "the clouds gathered thick upon us, and the winds singing and whistling most unusually" cause them to cast off the small unnamed ketch they are towing. William Strachey continues:

> [A] dreadful storm and hideous began to blow from out [of] the northeast, which swelling and roaring, as it were, by fits, some hours with more violence than others, at length did beat all light from heaven, which like an hell of darkness turned black upon us ... the terrible cries and murmurs of the winds ... such unmerciful tempest ... that it worketh upon the whole ... body, and most loathsomely affecteth all the powers thereof.

For four and twenty hours the storm in a restless tumult had blown so exceedingly as we could not apprehend in our imaginations any possibility of greater violence. Yet did we still find it not only more terrible but more constant, fury added to fury, and one storm urging a second more outrageous than the former ....

It could not be said to rain. The waters like whole rivers did flood in the air.... Winds and seas were as mad as fury and rage could make them. For mine own part, I had been in some storms before ... upon the coast of Barbary and Algier ... and ... in the Adriatic Gulf.... Yet all that I had ever suffered gathered together might not hold comparison with this. There was not a moment in which the sudden splitting or instant oversetting of the ship was not expected.

Howbeit this was not all. It pleased God to bring a greater affliction yet upon us, for in the beginning of the storm we had received ... a mighty leak, and the ship in every joint almost having spewed out her oakum before we were aware.

THE SHIP LEAKS AND TAKES ON MORE THAN FIVE FEET OF WATER

A sailing ship like the *Sea Venture* is built by laying planks next to and overlapping each other. The spaces or joints between them are caulked or filled with a tar and fiber material called oakum. Strachey relates that they have five feet of water above the ballast and are in danger of sinking. Crewmen with candles search the hold for leaks and can't find any holes, just the leaking joints.

SEPARATED FROM THE FLEET

The *Sea Venture* loses contact with all the other ships of the fleet in the first day. They cut loose the ketch on the fear that the ketch will swamp and pull both ships under, and the ketch and those aboard are never heard from again.

The other six ships emerge from the storm after 48 hours. Eventually all six of the other ships and the *Virginia*, which had turned back and started again after repairs, all reach Jamestown in good time. Only the *Sea Venture* is blown along with the storm and endures much, much more.

ALL MEN INCLUDING GENTLEMEN BAIL OR PUMP

On Tuesday morning, Governor Gates divides all the crew and passengers, including gentlemen and except for the women, totaling 140, into three groups in the front, middle, and rear of the ship. John Rolfe, along with the others, is to either bail with buckets or operate the pumps in shifts of one hour of work alternating with one hour of rest. John Rolfe and the others do this for the next 72 hours as the ship rolls and pitches. This is an extraordinary measure, as gentlemen not only aren't used to but don't do manual labor. So the Governor's requirement that all men participate equally was a desperate move.

Strachey continues: "The men might be seen to labor … for life, and the better sort, even our governor and admiral themselves, not refusing their turn.…" They work "with tired bodies and wasted spirits" for three days and nights. Strachey continues: "During all this time, the heavens looked so black upon us that it was not possible" to see a star at night or a sunbeam by day.

ST. ELMO'S FIRE

On Thursday night, the fourth night, Admiral Sir George Somers is on watch. He sees:

> a little round light like a faint star, trembling and streaming along with a sparkling blaze half the height upon the mainmast, and shooting sometimes from shroud to shroud ….

For half the night it keeps up, "running sometimes along the main yard to the very end, and then returning…" Admiral Somers calls many people to observe with him what is called St. Elmo's fire. They take it as a good omen. In the morning, Friday morning, it disappears.

NOW TEN FEET OF WATER IN THE HOLD

They throw overboard much luggage, beer, oil, cider, wine, vinegar, and all the cannon on the starboard side. The men are very tired, having worked from Tuesday until Friday morning without sleep or food. And at Friday noon there is now ten feet of water above the ballast, twice the depth on Tuesday. Strachey says there is a "general determination" to shut the hatches, commend their souls to God, and commit the ship to the mercy of the seas.

Another passenger, Silvester Jourdain describes it thus:

> … we were taken with a most sharp and cruel storm …which did not only separate us from the residue of our fleet … but with the violent working of the seas our ship became so shaken, torn, and leaked that she received so much water as covered two tier of hogsheads above the ballast; that our men stood up to the middles with buckets … and kettles to bail out the water and continually pumped for three days and three nights together without any intermission; and yet the water seemed rather to increase than to diminish. Insomuch that all our men, being utterly spent … were even resolved, without any hope of their lives … to have committed themselves to the mercy of the sea … seeing no help nor hope … that [they] would escape … present sinking.

FAREWELL MY FRIENDS

Jourdain relates that those who have a private stock of alcoholic beverages fetch it and toast their friends and take leave of them until they meet again in the next world.

LAND! THE DEVIL'S ISLES

Around noon on Friday, July 28, 1609, Admiral Sir George Somers who is on watch and has been for three days and three nights cries "Land." Admiral Somers and Captain Newport know where they were, and it is not good. They have been blown by the tempest near an area we now call the Bermuda Triangle and are approaching the dangerous and dreaded islands they know as the Devil's Isles.

These islands are uninhabited and more feared and avoided by sea travelers than any other place in the world. The Devil's Isles are legendary in that it is known that all who go there have terrible experiences. Besides shipwreck, there are tempests, thunders, and fearful things seen and heard.

As they approach the shore of the islands, the boatswain takes soundings, measurements of the depth of the sea by dropping a weighted rope over the side that is knotted every six feet. Each knot is a fathom, and the boatswain counts the knots as he lets out the line. First it is thirteen fathoms, then seven fathoms, then four fathoms. Finally everyone knows why the islands are uninhabited and feared, as no ship has ever landed or anchored safely in these waters because of a massive reef encircling the islands. There are the remains of many ships wrecked on the reef.

SHIPWRECKED

The *Sea Venture* tries to get through the reef to safe anchorage, but fails. One-half mile off shore, the *Sea Venture* hits the reef, hard. Fortunately in unfortunate circumstances, she becomes wedged between two large rocks on the reef and will not budge. Luckily, the *Sea Venture* is upright and held fast in place, and not banging or breaking apart against the rocks. This allows use of the longboats to get all 153 people safely ashore, and the ship's dog and their pigs too. Since the ship is still sitting there, they go back for all the remaining provisions which haven't been thrown overboard, then the rigging, then all the iron used to build the ship, then the masts, and finally some planking.

CASTAWAY ON A DESERTED ISLAND
At least the storm has abated and they have survived due to courageous leadership and hard work against all odds. But now they are shipwrecked and castaway on an uninhabited, deserted island that all mariners fear in the Bermuda Triangle.

Ironically, the day they become castaways, July 28, 1609, goes down in history as the date of the first settlement of Bermuda. But for the castaways, it's still the Devil's Isles.

SHAKESPEARE
Eventually, William Strachey's account of the tempest, castaways on a deserted island, and St. Elmo's fire will be circulated around London and inspire *The Tempest* by William Shakespeare.

RISK
John Rolfe knew there was risk involved in his first ocean crossing and also in the colony of Virginia from disease and Indian attack. He accepted and embraced that risk and took his wife along. He probably didn't think much about the risk of a tempest, a storm yes, but a tempest, no. I imagine shipwreck was far from an expected risk. And castaway on a deserted island for nearly 10 months, he probably didn't imagine. Yet John Rolfe accepted all the risks, both expected and unexpected, and continued on after disaster.

MEANWHILE, ELSEWHERE, THIS IS HAPPENING ...

In Jamestown, between August 11 and August 14, 1609, the other seven ships of the Third Supply arrive. Captain Gabriel Archer on the *Blessing* reports that they were in high winds and seas for about 44 hours, less than half of the more than 96 hours that the *Sea Venture* endured. The *Sea Venture* doesn't arrive and is thought lost.

The other seven ships of the Third Supply add about 400 settlers to Jamestown.

Chapter 3

FROM DEVIL'S ISLES TO PARADISE

HIDEOUS SCREECHING

As night falls, the castaways on the beach are very afraid. Many hideous screeches come from the brush and trees. When a man goes to investigate, he is swarmed by birds, often landing on his head and shoulders and screeching. The castaways are terrified. These nocturnal ground-nesting seabirds are called Cahows because of their eerie cries. We now call them Bermuda Petrels.

In the 1620's, Cahows are believed to be extinct, a belief that persists for 330 years. In 1951, eighteen breeding pairs will be discovered on a remote part of Bermuda. The Cahow or Bermuda Petrel is now the national bird of Bermuda.

EASY FOOD

During the day, wild pigs, perhaps attracted by the pigs saved from the ship, rampage through the rude shelters which the *Sea Venture* passengers and crew have constructed on the beach. Once the marooned castaways get used to the eerie and rampaging island inhabitants, they see the pigs and the Cahows as an easy source of food. And the fishing in the lagoon is good. Tropical fruits too.

PARADISE?

Before long, the castaways begin to see the Devil's Isles differently. Yes there are storms, but the weather and climate are generally good. Food is abundant and easy to come by. Fresh water is available. They even plant some English crops that grow well. The transformation from the scary shipwreck and first night where the birds attack those who wander off the beach and screech through the night, to the easy paradise of plentiful food and water of several weeks later is extremely dramatic. They surely thank their God for this transformation.

TOBACCO

The castaways find a stand of tobacco on a hill on one island. Maybe John Rolfe gathers some tobacco seeds in Bermuda. I haven't been able to determine which variety of tobacco was growing there at that time. Today this area is called Tobacco Bay, St. George's Island, Bermuda.

MANY ISLANDS

The castaways discover that Bermuda is not one island, but quite a few small islands very close together. In fact, Bermuda consists of 181 islands with a total area of 20.6 square miles or 53.3 square kilometers. That's the size of a square about 4.5 miles to a side. Or a little smaller in area than the area of Manhattan in New York City, which is 23 square miles. And it's only about a third of the area of present-day Richmond, Virginia, at 62.5 square miles.

SENDING A BOAT TO VIRGINIA TO BRING BACK HELP

About a month after the shipwreck, on Monday August 28, 1609, Governor Gates sends a longboat rigged with a sail with Master's Mate Henry Ravens and six other sailors and one merchant named Thomas Whittingham to Virginia to bring back a ship large enough to rescue all the castaways. They expect the voyage to take a week or so each way. Governor Gates has signal fires built every night for two months on the top of a hill to guide their rescuers back to Bermuda. Later reports are that Ravens and the others reach the American shore but are immediately killed by Indians.

After two months the castaways realize that help probably isn't coming from Virginia and that they will have to do something else if they want to leave Bermuda. Therein is the problem.

STAY OR GO?

The leaders, of course, know it is their duty to go to Jamestown and assist with the colonization and success of the colony. The colonists have heard of the hardships of Jamestown and like the ease of life on Bermuda. And one colony is as good as another, isn't it? Many people want to stay on Bermuda rather than continue to Jamestown. I believe John Rolfe stayed focused and faithful to his entrepreneurial goal of growing tobacco in Virginia and wanted to continue on to Virginia even with the terrible obstacles he was facing.

BUILDING A SHIP, THE *DELIVERANCE*

With no prospect of rescue and no one else knowing where they are or even that they are alive, in

October 1609, Governor Thomas Gates sets his shipwright Richard Frobisher and four carpenters to building a ship to take the castaways to Virginia. It is to be named the *Deliverance* in obvious hope that it would deliver them from their castaway situation. It is 40 feet on the keel and 60 feet overall. They use the salvaged parts of the *Sea Venture* as much as possible.

BUILDING ANOTHER SHIP, THE *PATIENCE*

When Admiral Somers realizes the *Deliverance* isn't large enough to carry all the castaways in one trip, he proposes, on November 27, 1609, building a second ship. Governor Gates gives him two carpenters and 20 other men and Somers sets up operations across the bay on another island. That ship, to be named the *Patience*, is 29 feet on the keel. The only salvaged material Governor Gates makes available to Admiral Somers for building the *Patience* is a single iron bolt.

ROMANCE AND MARRIAGE ON BERMUDA

In November 1609, Reverend Bucke marries Elizabeth Persons, Mistress Horton's maid, and Thomas Powell, Admiral Somers' cook. This is the first marriage on Bermuda. Today many couples have a destination wedding on Bermuda, and many others honeymoon there.

MURDER AND MUTINY NUMBER ONE

Paradise creates its own problems. In general, some think Bermuda too much like paradise to leave for the uncertainty and likely hardships of Jamestown. Five separate mutinies challenge the leadership and the leaders' plans to go on to Jamestown.

Two sailors get into an argument, and one of them, Robert Waters, bashes the other, Edward Samuel, in the head with a shovel, killing Samuel. Robert Waters, no relation to Admiral Somers' assistant Edward Waters, is arrested and sentenced to hang the next morning. He is tied to a tree overnight and several guards stationed. When the guards supposedly fall asleep, some sailors cut the ropes binding Waters, take Waters into the woods, and hide him. The friends of Robert Waters feed him daily, and Waters remains out of sight of the search parties. Murder by one sailor has turned into mutiny by other sailors. Eventually, an appeal for leniency to Governor Gates results in a pardon.

MUTINY NUMBER TWO
The second mutiny involves John Want, Christopher Carter, Nicholas Bennett, and three other men. They want to set up their own settlement on a different island. Governor Gates decides to let them do it, so he chooses an island and has the six men put there without provisions. They soon tire of their solitude and likely their hunger. After many pleas for forgiveness, Gates allows them to come back.

MUTINY NUMBER THREE, AIN'T TOO PROUD TO BEG
The third mutiny is by Samuel Hopkins, a radical Puritan protestant layman, who claims that Governor Gates and the other leaders have no authority over anyone since the shipwreck. He wants to stay on Bermuda and enjoy its ease rather than have to go to Virginia and possible hardship. The other castaways he tries to recruit report him to Governor Gates. Gates sentences Hopkins to death in January 1610. Hopkins pleads and begs for mercy and cites the hardship his

death would have on his wife and children back in England. Captain Newport and William Strachey prevail on Governor Gates to pardon Hopkins. Samuel Hopkins later will gain fame as one of the passengers, along with his family, on the *Mayflower* in 1620.

MUTINY NUMBER FOUR

The fourth mutiny, on March 13, 1610, involves Henry Paine who refuses his guard duty, attacks his commander, and proclaims that the Governor has no authority over him. He is tried, convicted, and sentenced to be hanged immediately. He pleads for his life, but the Governor has pardoned so many men that it is difficult to keep order. His pleas for his life are denied, but his plea as a gentleman to be shot rather than hanged, which is considered a more honorable way to die, is granted.

MUTINY NUMBER FIVE

When Henry Paine is executed, his co-conspirators take to the woods fearing that Paine has named them as co-conspirators. Paine was one of a large group of men who conspired to steal the castaways' supplies and weapons and kill Governor Gates and all of Gates supporters, so that they could stay on Bermuda. The leaders are Robert Waters and Christopher Carter, both veterans of other mutinies. Admiral Somers convinces all but two, Christopher Carter and Robert Waters, to return to the group. Those two escape and hide from the authorities.

SARAH ROLFE GIVES BIRTH TO BERMUDA ROLFE

Sarah Rolfe gives birth on February 11, 1610 to a baby girl, the first child for Sarah and John Rolfe. The baby is christened Bermuda by Reverend Richard Bucke, with Captain Christopher Newport, Mistress Horton, and William Strachey as witnesses. Bermuda Rolfe is the first person born on Bermuda.

Bermuda Rolfe dies several days later and is buried on Bermuda. This tragic personal loss was another terrible setback for John Rolfe. It must have affected him deeply.

In March 1610, the wife of Edward Eason gives birth to a baby girl. She is christened Bermudas, and Captain Newport and William Strachey are witnesses.

DEATHS ON BERMUDA
Three of the castaways, Jeffrey Briars, Richard Lewis, and William Hitchman, die of natural causes. As we saw, one sailor, Robert Waters, murdered another, Edward Samuel, and one castaway, Henry Paine, was executed for sedition.

THE *DELIVERANCE* AND THE *PATIENCE* ARE LAUNCHED
On March 30, 1610, after eight months on Bermuda, the *Deliverance* is launched and towed to a sheltered mooring where it will be rigged and loaded with ballast and supplies.

In late April 1610, the *Patience* is launched.

MACHUMPS MURDERS NAMONTACK
One of the two Indians returning to Virginia on the *Sea Venture*, Machumps, murders the other, Namontack, on Bermuda. Somehow, this isn't noticed at the time and isn't noticed until they reach Virginia.

140 CASTAWAYS REMAIN

Of the 153 castaways landed on Bermuda, eight left in the small boat for Virginia and were never seen again, three died of natural causes, one sailor named Edward Samuel was murdered by Robert Waters, one Indian, Namontack, was murdered, and one castaway was executed. That reduces the number to 139. Add the baby Bermudas Eason and the total is 140 to be transported to Virginia.

TWO FUGITIVES STAY ON BERMUDA

The two fugitive mutineers, Christopher Carter and Edward Waters, both of whom have been involved in previous mutinies, hide out and refuse to go to Virginia.

138 CASTAWAYS LEAVE BERMUDA

Thus only 138 people leave Bermuda for Virginia on May 10, 1610, in the *Patience*, captained by Admiral George Somers, and the *Deliverance*, captained by Christopher Newport. John and Sarah Rolfe are on the *Deliverance* with Admiral Somers and Governor Gates. They have been marooned on Bermuda for nearly ten months.

The *Deliverance* tries to get through the same part of the reef where the *Sea Venture* was stuck. They mark the channel and think they can get over the reef because the smaller ship sits higher in the water than the *Sea Venture*. Nevertheless, they run aground on soft coral. After pulling the *Deliverance* off the soft coral, they are able to get through the reef. The *Patience* sits even higher in the water and has no trouble getting through the V shaped gap in the reef that had snared the *Sea Venture*.

MEANWHILE, ELSEWHERE, THIS IS HAPPENING …

On August 28, 1609, Henry Hudson is the first European to see Delaware Bay. Though English, he sails for the Dutch East India Company and the Netherlands. His ship is the *Halve Maen* or *Half Moon*.

On September 3, 1609, Henry Hudson enters the estuary of the Hudson River near what is today New York City. The estuary was discovered by Giovanni da Verrazzano in 1524. On September 12, 1609, Hudson discovers and sails up the Hudson River for ten days to what is now Albany, for the Dutch, which leads to the Netherlands claiming the surrounding area, including New Amsterdam, now New York City.

On September 10, 1609, John Smith is returning from a trip to the falls of the James River near what is now Richmond, and is sleeping in his boat. He later wrote that "accidentally, one fired his powder bag." Apparently, one of his companions lighted it. He got a serious burn on his body and thigh, an area about nine or ten inches square. To quench the fire, Smith jumps overboard into the river and has to be saved from drowning. Since a powder bag doesn't catch fire by itself, it is often speculated that the other men on the boat lit it in an effort to rid themselves of the contentious John Smith, but didn't have the stomach to let him drown or hit him in the head with an oar and drown him.

Because of the severity of his gunpowder burns, and perhaps because he has narrowly escaped death three times at the hands of his own countrymen, on October 4, 1609, John Smith resigns and leaves Virginia and returns to England in one of the ships which survived the tempest that wrecked the *Sea Venture*. The Powhatan Indians are told Smith died from his wounds.

Smith never returns to Jamestown or Virginia. He does, however, go to New England and map the area in 1614 and again in 1615.

In March 1610, Galileo Galilei publishes a short treatise titled *Starry Messenger* about his observations with a telescope. He sees the moon and the stars, and he proves that the Milky Way is a large number of stars. From January 7-13, 1610, he discovers four moons of Jupiter which he names Io, Europa, Ganymede, and Calisto. Galileo says he can see ten times as many stars with his telescope as with the naked eye. Although the telescope was invented in 1608 in the Netherlands by Hans Lippershey, in 1609 Galileo takes the idea and improves upon it by making a telescope with 3x magnification. He later makes one with 30x magnification. Galileo, who is at the time a mathematician at the University of Padua in the Veneto region near Venice, desires to return to his home city of Florence and so dedicates his treatise to Cosimo II de Medici, the Grand Duke of Tuscany, hoping to gain patronage in Florence, which he eventually does.

In 1610, Princess Pocahontas, daughter of Wahunsenaca, Chief Powhatan, marries a warrior named Kocoum, the younger brother of Chief Japazaw of the

Potowomac tribe on the Potomac River. Princess Pocahontas and Kocoum live in the Potowomac village.

On May 14, 1610, King Henri IV of France is assassinated by a fanatical Catholic. He was born on December 13, 1553. He became King of Navarre in 1572, a position he held until his death. He converted to Catholicism before being crowned King of France on August 2, 1589. He was a popular king and ruled for over 20 years. He is known for the Edict of Nantes which he enacted in 1598 guaranteeing religious freedom to Protestants, effectively ending a civil war. He is the first of the Bourbon line of monarchs.

Chapter 4

TERROR AND TRAGEDY, RATHER THAN DELIVERANCE

AMERICA, AND THE WORLD, WILL CHANGE
America: The Story of Us is a 2010 production of the History Channel. It begins the story of America with a segment that names only one man, John Rolfe.

> One ship, the *Deliverance*, carries a cargo that will change America forever. On board is John Rolfe, a 24 year old English farmer. Ambitious, self-reliant, visionary, a born entrepreneur.

HELL ON EARTH
On May 21, 1610, the *Deliverance* and the *Patience* reach the Chesapeake Bay. It takes two more days to reach Jamestown. So on May 23, 1610, a year and eight days after leaving London, John Rolfe disembarks at Jamestown expecting to find a reasonably successful functioning colony. The History Channel's 2010 production *America: The Story of Us* continues:

> North America is the ultimate land of opportunity. A continent of vast untapped wealth, starting with the most valuable

resource of all, land…. The settlers expect nothing less than Eldorado. But what Rolfe finds at the English settlement at Jamestown is Hell on Earth.

This is not the deliverance Rolfe is expecting. He knows circumstances will be more difficult than on Bermuda, but no one expects what he finds. He and his *Sea Venture* companions expected a functional fort with hundreds of settlers and food enough for everyone. John Rolfe undoubtedly expects to start his tobacco planting.

Instead, John Rolfe finds the stockade and houses in total disrepair. Settlers have scavenged the wood to burn to keep themselves warm, leaving the stockade and houses in poor shape and with missing parts. William Strachey describes it thus:

> Viewing the fort, we found the palisades torn down, the ports open, the gates from off the hinges, and empty houses, which [the] owners' death had taken from them, rent up and burnt, rather than the dwellers would step into the woods a stone's cast off from them to fetch other firewood. And it is true the Indian killed as fast without, if our men stirred but beyond the bounds of their blockhouse, as famine and pestilence did within …

Even worse, John Rolfe sees that there are only 60 settlers remaining in Jamestown, and they are emaciated to the point of looking like scarecrows. They have seen hundreds of their fellows die, and they are near death themselves. There had been over 350 settlers in

November 1609, just six months before, and over 500 settlers in the summer of 1609.

Instead of heaven on earth, plenty of food, a life of relative ease, and friendly natives as the Virginia Company of London advertised when seeking settlers for Virginia, John Rolfe and the *Sea Venture* survivors find famine, illness, cannibalism, mutiny, and war with the Indians, a war the settlers are losing.

INDIAN WAR

Relations with the Indians have deteriorated to a state of open warfare. Any settlers who stray outside the stockade to hunt or forage for food or firewood are attacked with bows and arrows or tomahawks and killed. Eventually few have the courage to leave the fort, as scores have been killed. Several days before Rolfe's arrival, two settlers are killed outside the fort, and shortly after Rolfe steps ashore another two are killed.

When it becomes obvious in the fall of 1609 that Jamestown will struggle to feed all its settlers, a contingent of adventurers is sent further upriver to settle and find their own food sources. Many of them are killed by Indians and the survivors return to Jamestown. Another contingent is sent down river to a lookout fort on the Chesapeake at Point Comfort for the same reason. They immediately lose many of their number to Indian attack, but 30-40 survive the winter.

BETRAYAL BY THE *SWALLOW*

The *Swallow* is one of the seven ships that already arrived in Jamestown from the *Sea Venture* fleet. It is sent to trade for food with friendlier tribes for the colony. It is now under the command of Francis West, younger brother of Sir Thomas West, Lord De La Warr, who would later be appointed Governor for Life of Virginia and come to Jamestown, embarrassed by his younger brother's actions. Francis West trades for supplies for a hungry Jamestown with a tribe not allied with the Powhatan tribes, then mutinies, takes the much needed supplies, abandons the other colonists, and sails for England against orders. This results in a loss of precious food and 37 men from the colony.

THE STARVING TIME

The winter of 1609-1610 is known as the Starving Time. Indians kill settlers who stray out of the stockade. There is no food. The settlers eat their livestock, dogs, then rats and anything that moves. Finally they boil their shoe leather and leather belts so that they are soft enough to chew. Some settlers dig up dead bodies and eat the flesh of their dead fellows. The 60 settlers who survive are only 17% of the 350 settlers who started the winter just six months before.

Perhaps John Rolfe realizes that if the *Sea Venture* hadn't been shipwrecked, the vast majority of its passengers also would have perished in Jamestown just like the settlers who reached Jamestown on the other seven ships. Indeed, the torturous *Sea Venture* shipwreck may have been a blessing in disguise.

ENGLISH CANNIBAL

Shortly before the *Sea Venture* survivors arrive in Jamestown, an Englishman had been caught after killing his pregnant wife whom he planned to eat. He was burned at the stake. Cannibalism! By an Englishman, not a native.

DROUGHT

A seven year drought had started in 1607, so the Indians have no corn to trade even if they are willing to do so, and it is planting time, not harvest time, when the *Sea Venture* survivors arrive. The settlers have no food seeds, and no strength to plant even if they had the seeds.

The settlers have lost or ruined any fishing nets and fishing lines they previously had, so can catch no fish from the James River. Hunting is impossible, as the Indians kill any settlers who leave the safety of Jamestown's fort.

PLEASE, PLEASE, LET'S GO HOME TO ENGLAND

The emaciated settlers who survived the Starving Time and are themselves near death from starving, urge Governor Gates to take them home to England. The castaways from Bermuda have only a few weeks of supplies on board their two small ships. They didn't expect to have to feed everyone until the non-existent fall harvest, and can't do so.

Finally, on June 6, 1610, Gates tells everyone to prepare for leaving Jamestown. He plans to sail to Newfoundland in overcrowded vessels. There they will find fishing boats and be able to get supplies and alleviate the crowding by putting some of the settlers on fishing boats for the return trip to England. Preparations for leaving include burying the fort's cannons just inside the gates of the fort so that the Indians won't have easy access to them.

It will be a tight fit on the four small ships. There are the 138 survivors from Bermuda that arrived on the

Deliverance and the *Patience*. Then there are the 60 survivors in Jamestown itself. Plus 30-40 men who had survived the winter at Point Comfort on the Chesapeake, for a total of 230-240 people.

HOMEWARD BOUND ON FOUR SHIPS

General Gates joins Captain Christopher Newport on the *Deliverance*, Admiral Somers commands the *Patience*, Captain George Percy commands the *Discovery*, and Captain James Davies, who has met the Bermuda survivors at Point Comfort, commands the *Virginia*. General Gates posts guards to prevent the survivors of the Starving Time from burning the hated fort that has cost them so much grief. Gates makes sure he is the last to board the ships.

At about noon on June 7, 1610, the four ships sail down the James River on the way back to England. After sailing as far down river as the tide and wind will take them that day, they anchor for the night at Mulberry Island in the James River.

FAILURE AND RESILIENCE

After a life threatening tempest and ten months stranded on a wild island, the *Sea Venture* and John Rolfe have finally reached their destination and face death for the second time, this time in Jamestown. Now they have to abandon Jamestown because of the dire conditions there with no hope of salvation. The Virginia colony has failed, and with it John Rolfe's entrepreneurial plans, at least for the time being. Rolfe can hope that a future expedition from England to Virginia will allow him to come back and carry out his vision. Because of the commitment to his vision he has already shown, I believe John Rolfe was resilient enough to take it in stride and plan for the future.

MEANWHILE, ELSEWHERE, THIS IS HAPPENING …

On July 18, 1610, Italian painter Caravaggio dies. He was born September 28, 1573.

In 1610, the first commercial shipment of tea from China, green tea it was, goes to Europe in a Dutch ship. Tea drinking spreads from the Netherlands to the rest of Europe over the next few decades.

Chapter 5

SURPRISE! GOOD SURPRISE OR BAD SURPRISE?

FOURTH SUPPLY FLEET SAILS FROM ENGLAND

On April 1, 1610, a Fourth Supply fleet is dispatched from England, from Cowes on the Isle of Wight just off the southernmost coast of England. It includes a new Governor to replace General Gates who was thought lost and dead in the tempest or hurricane.

VIRGINIA'S NEW GOVERNOR FOR LIFE LORD DE LA WARR

Sir Thomas West, Lord De La Warr (later spelled Delaware), is appointed Governor for Life and sails on the flagship of the fleet, the *De La Warr*. The vice admiral ship is the *Blessing*, a survivor of the 1609 tempest, which had returned to England, and is the smallest of the three ships. The *Hercules* is the rear admiral. Between them they carry 150 settlers, plus sailors and supplies for 400 men for a full year.

The little fleet sails south to the Azores, arriving April 12 and anchoring. The next day a storm arises, the anchor cables break and anchors are lost, and the ships are forced to sail into the storm. On April 14, the

Hercules is separated from the rest of the fleet as they are sailing west in the storm.

On April 27, the *De La Warr* and the *Blessing* turn north towards Virginia.

DE LA WARR REACHES THE CHESAPEAKE

By a strange coincidence, on June 7, 1610, the same day General Gates and the settlers including Rolfe leave Jamestown, Lord De La Warr's fleet anchors off Point Comfort in the Chesapeake. From the men at Point Comfort Governor De La Warr learns that General Gates and Admiral Somers are both safe and in Jamestown.

STRANGE ENCOUNTER

The next day, June 8, 1610, before the departing settlers leave Mulberry Island, they are probably waiting for the tide to turn, Lord De La Warr's fleet, probably riding the incoming tide, meets the departing fleet of Acting Governor Sir Thomas Gates.

SURPRISE! GO BACK TO JAMESTOWN

Governor for Life Lord De La Warr informs Gates of his leadership position and the ample supplies he carries. He orders the departing settlers back to Jamestown. It must have been a mind blowing encounter.

Most settlers are sorely disappointed that day. John Rolfe, however, needs to stay in Virginia to achieve his entrepreneurial goals. With the new supplies, his faith in his vision, his committed decision, and his plan are rewarded.

LORD DE LA WARR IN CHARGE OF JAMESTOWN

On June 10, 1610, Lord De La Warr and the others arrive in Jamestown. On June 12, Governor De La Warr announces his staff appointments. His Council consists of Sir Thomas Gates, now lieutenant general, Sir George Somers, still admiral, George Percy, who becomes captain of Jamestown's 50 man garrison, Sir Ferdinando Wainman, who has come over with De La Warr as master of ordnance, Christopher Newport, remaining as vice admiral, and William Strachey as Secretary.

On June 13, De La Warr calls a meeting of his council to discuss the situation of Jamestown. They have enough grain, but no fresh meat or fish. Admiral Sir George Somers volunteers to return to Bermuda to obtain fish, turtles, and hogs.

SARAH ROLFE DIES

Within weeks after returning to Jamestown, Sarah Rolfe, John Rolfe's wife, dies. The hardships she had experienced were apparently beyond her endurance. What a roller coaster ride for John Rolfe. The colony now seems to be saved, but his wife dies. This is a second tragic personal loss that has to take a toll on Rolfe.

ADMIRAL SOMERS RETURNS TO BERMUDA TO GET FOOD FOR JAMESTOWN

On Wednesday, June 20, 1610, Lord De La Warr sends Captain Argall and Sir George Somers to Bermuda to bring back some wild hogs and other edibles for the Jamestown colony. Admiral Somers in the *Patience* and Captain Samuel Argall in the *Discovery* sail down the

James River on a journey to Bermuda to secure provisions. They expect to be back in Jamestown by mid-August. This same Captain Samuel Argall will later figure prominently in John Rolfe's story.

Sailing out the mouth of the Chesapeake Bay, they encounter dense fog and unfavorable winds that delay them for weeks and finally separate them.

INDIAN WAR

A few days after Somers and Argall leave for Bermuda, hostilities break out with the Indians. The Indians are doubtless disturbed by all the new arrivals. Sir Thomas Gates goes to Fort Algernon at Point Comfort. He discovers that the longboat belonging to the fort has broken loose from its mooring and blown across the James River. He sends one Humphrey Blunt in an old canoe to retrieve it. When Blunt arrives on the far shore, a group of Nansemond Indians kill him.

Then, on July 9, 1610, Sir Thomas Gates, deputy Governor, leads a raiding party to revenge Blunt's death. They go to Kecoughtan, an Indian village about four miles from Fort Algernon at Point Comfort, on the north shore of the James River. William Strachey and George Percy write descriptions of the raid. The English destroy the village and build Fort Charles on the site.

DEPUTY GOVERNOR GATES LEAVES FOR ENGLAND

On July 20, 1610, Sir Thomas Gates sails for England on the *Blessing* to report to the Virginia Company of London and to attempt to secure more financial and logistical support for Jamestown. He carries William Strachey's 25,000 word narrative in the form of a letter addressed to "Excellent Lady," probably Lady Sara Smythe, wife of Sir Thomas Smythe, treasurer of the Virginia Company of London. The title of the narrative is *A True Reportory of the Wreck and Redemption of Sir Thomas Gates, Knight, upon and from the Islands of the Bermudas: His Coming to Virginia and the Estate of that Colony Then and After, under the Government of the Lord De La Warre, July 15, 1610, Written by William Strachey, Esquire.*

WILLIAM SHAKESPEARE'S *THE TEMPEST*

Strachey's very long letter has a famous place in history. It is circulated among interested parties in London. The story of the tempest and shipwreck of the *Sea Venture* on a deserted island inspires and even supplies some verbal, plot, and thematic elements for the London playwright, William Shakespeare, for a new play called *The Tempest. The Tempest* will be first performed on November 1, 1611 for King James I and Queen Anne at Whitehall Palace.

GROW TOBACCO NEXT YEAR

Because of the state of the colony and its need for repairs, and because it was already late in the growing season, John Rolfe can not start his tobacco experiments in the summer of 1610.

CAPTAIN ARGALL BRINGS COD FROM NEW ENGLAND

In September 1610, Captain Samuel Argall is back in Jamestown with the *Discovery* and a load of cod from New England to help feed the colonists.

ADMIRAL SOMERS DIES ON BERMUDA

On November 9, 1610, Sir George Somers dies on Bermuda where he has sailed with his nephew Matthew Somers on the *Patience*. Admiral Somers has asked Matthew to bury him on Bermuda, then return to Jamestown with the provisions they gathered, and then to go to England to tell Mrs. Somers of his death and to raise money to colonize Bermuda.

PICKLED

Matthew Somers instead eviscerates his uncle's corpse and buries his heart and entrails on St. George's Island, Bermuda. He then secretly packs and pickles the rest of his uncle's corpse to take to England in a barrel without the knowledge of the crew because sailors consider a corpse on board a ship to be bad luck. Matthew Somers is now Captain of the *Patience*. Finally, in late March or early April 1611, Captain Matthew Somers and the *Patience* leave Bermuda for England, not Jamestown, with the pickled body of Sir George Somers.

Because of Admiral Somers' nephew's betrayal, Jamestown never receives the provisions from Bermuda that Governor De La Warr sent Admiral Somers to get.

DEALING WITH OBSTACLES, SETBACKS, AND DISAPPOINTMENTS

Since boarding the Sea Venture on May 15, 1609, John Rolfe has had more than his share of obstacles, setbacks, disappointments, and tragic personal loss. Yet he had a strong religious faith and he carried on with his vision and entrepreneurial plan.

For John Rolfe, the difference between the spring of 1610 at the end of the Starving Time when he arrived in Jamestown and the spring of 1611 must have been like the difference between night and day.

BIRTH OF POCAHONTAS' FIRST CHILD, LITTLE KOCOUM

In 1611, Princess Pocahontas, who will become a very important person to John Rolfe and Jamestown, gives birth to a son known as Little Kocoum, named after his father, Kocoum, probably in the native village of Potowomac.

MEANWHILE, ELSEWHERE, THIS IS HAPPENING ...

On May 2, 1611, the Authorized Version of the *Bible*, now known as the King James Version, is first published in London by printer Robert Barker. It is an English translation by the Church of England that was begun in January 1604 at the direction of King James I.

Chapter 6

JOHN ROLFE'S CASH CROP SAVES THE COLONY

THE VIRGINIA COLONY IS FAILING

The Virginia Company of London has three goals for the colony, gold, glory, and God. They are failing at all three.

Aside from the Virginia colony's struggles with physical survival due to disease, lack of food, and armed conflict with the natives, it is also failing financially. The investors in London have seen no financial return and see no prospects of any future return.

The adventurers have found no gold or silver. Their initial expectation of conquering the natives and taking their gold and silver and forcing them to mine more hasn't worked out. The Virginia adventurers want to follow the example of the Spanish in Mexico, with Hernán Cortés conquering the Aztecs in 1521, and in Peru, with Francisco Pizarro beginning subjugation of the Incas in 1533. There is no gold or silver in Virginia. The fallback of taking pearls from the natives hasn't worked out either. There are no pearls in Virginia.

FOOL'S GOLD

The colonists have sent to England on two separate occasions ships full of ore that is supposed to contain gold, but it turns out to be worthless iron pyrite or fool's gold. They also ship back cedar timber, clapboards, and sassafras, and set up a glass foundry (even if there were sufficient raw materials and craftsmen to make enough glass, imagine the breakage in shipping glass items to England).

The investors in England are becoming greatly concerned about the lack of financial success of the venture.

CONVERTING THE NATIVES TO PROTESTANTISM

The God goal of the venture, although obviously of subsidiary importance to the financial goal, is to bring the Protestant version of God to the natives. They hope to convert them to good Protestant Christians for their own good and to prevent them from later being converted by the Spanish, who were converting natives in the Caribbean, to Catholic Christianity. The English colonists have made virtually no progress in converting the natives to Christianity.

GLORY

So far there has been no glory for the company or for any individuals involved. The King has a colony, but it is failing, so there is no glory there.

JOHN ROLFE PLANTS TRINIDAD TOBACCO SEEDS

The financial future of the Virginia colony is about to change due to the efforts of one man. In 1611,

John Rolfe plants Trinidad tobacco seeds (Nicotiana tabacum). Both William Strachey, first recorder and Secretary of the Virginia colony, and Ralph Hamor, a later Secretary, credit Rolfe with experimenting with tobacco seeds from Trinidad. It's not recorded how he acquired the seeds, though it seems that such a well thought out entrepreneurial plan would have had seeds at the beginning. It is, however, possible that Rolfe acquired them on Bermuda, where the shipwreck survivors found tobacco growing, or acquired them by trade.

ROLFE SUCCESSFULLY PLANTS HIS FIRST TOBACCO CROP

Rolfe plants his first tobacco crop in 1611 and it grows successfully. The Trinidad tobacco grows about six feet tall, much taller than the three feet of the native tobacco (Nicotiana rustica).

LORD DE LA WARR RETURNS TO ENGLAND

Governor for Life De La Warr, who has been ill during most of his time in Jamestown, sails for home via Nevis in the Caribbean in an effort to recuperate from his illness. For some unexplained reason, he takes 50 extra men with him and thereby reduces the number of settlers. They are blown off course and land in the Azores. He finally arrives in England on June 11, 1611, and never returns to Virginia.

Captain George Percy takes over leadership of the colony on the departure of Lord De La Warr.

THE NEW ACTING GOVERNOR, SIR THOMAS DALE

Sir Thomas Dale arrives in Jamestown from London on May 19, 1611, with an additional 300 settlers. He is appointed Marshal of Virginia, the military head of the colony. He is also appointed Deputy Governor to Governor Sir Thomas Gates, who remains in England for the time being.

SPANISH SPIES

Also in May 1611, a Spanish ship on a spying mission from Cuba enters the Chesapeake Bay and Captain Don Diego de Molina and his pilot named Francis Lembry, a renegade Englishman masquerading as a Spaniard, go ashore and are captured by Captain James Davies, commander of the fort at Point Comfort and former Captain of the *Virginia* in the 1609 fleet. The ship carrying Molina and Lembry abandons them and sails away. The prisoners are taken to Jamestown. They are held prisoner for five years.

NEW GOVERNOR, SIR THOMAS GATES

In August 1611, Sir Thomas Gates returns as Governor with a fleet of nine ships and 280 new settlers and supplies. Sir Thomas Dale is Marshal still. Governor Gates has instructions to move the colony's headquarters farther upriver to some place less vulnerable to Spanish attack.

WILLIAM STRACHEY RETURNS TO ENGLAND, COINCIDENTALLY IN TIME FOR THE FIRST PERFORMANCE OF SHAKESPEARE'S *THE TEMPEST* WHICH HIS LETTER INSPIRED

On August 20, 1611, William Strachey leaves Jamestown on the ship *Prosperous* bound for England.

He arrives in London about the time of the first performance of *The Tempest*, by William Shakespeare, performed for King James I and Queen Anne at Whitehall Palace on All Saints' Day, November 1, 1611.

HENRICO, VIRGINIA

In September, Sir Thomas Dale and 350 men start building the town of Henrico (sometimes spelled Henricus) further upstream on the James River. On January 15, 1612, they complete the buildings and stockade of Henrico.

JOHN ROLFE'S FIRST SUCCESSFUL TOBACCO HARVEST

In the fall of 1611, John Rolfe has a successful harvest of his first tobacco crop of his Trinidad tobacco. He starts the curing process. He cuts the tobacco plants down and cures the tobacco by stripping the leaves from the stalks, throwing the leaves into a heap on the ground, and covering them with hay to help the process of fermentation. That method of curing tobacco sounds strange today, but that was the only way the English knew.

ENGLAND LIKES JOHN ROLFE'S TOBACCO

Early in 1612, John Rolfe ships to England a few hundred pounds of his Trinidad tobacco from his harvest of 1611 aboard the ship *Elizabeth* for evaluation by English merchants and smokers. Rolfe's tobacco is favorably received and reported as showing great promise. This feedback from his customers or potential customers is very valuable to Rolfe.

THE VIRGINIA COMPANY OF LONDON'S CHARTER NOW INCLUDES BERMUDA

The Virginia Company of London is granted a new charter on March 12, 1612. This new charter is a direct result of the *Sea Venture*'s shipwreck on Bermuda, as it includes Bermuda in the territory of the Virginias.

The islands are still officially the Somers Isles after Admiral George Somers who was in charge of the *Sea Venture* which shipwrecked on them in 1609. But the name Bermuda is commonly used both then and now. On April 28, 1612, the ship *Plough* with 60 colonists sails from London to colonize Bermuda along with the *Sea Venture* mutineers who had remained on the islands.

To honor its first inhabitants, the official flag and the official coat of arms of Bermuda to this day include a depiction of the shipwreck of the *Sea Venture*.

ROLFE ESTABLISHES VARINA FARMS NEAR HENRICO

In 1612, John Rolfe establishes a new plantation called Varina Farms across the river from Sir Thomas Dale's new Henrico settlement. Like most tobacco plantations, it was sited on the river to reduce transportation costs by exporting the tobacco directly from the wharf of the plantation.

JOHN ROLFE CROSS BREEDS TRINIDAD AND ORINOCO TOBACCO SEEDS

Rolfe acquires additional tobacco seeds from Caracas, Venezuela, the Orinoco type. He cross breeds Trinidad seeds with Orinoco seeds for his 1612 planting.

The years 1611 and 1612 are John Rolfe's period of experimentation, trial and error, with his tobacco crop. He isn't resting on his laurels, he's trying to improve his product. He sticks to his task even when he gets good feedback and he keeps improving his product and creating an even better mild tobacco that England craves. And, as John Rolfe always knew he would, he finally succeeds.

MEANWHILE, ELSEWHERE, THIS IS HAPPENING …

On May 10, 1612, in India, the man who designed and built the Taj Mahal, the future Shah Jahan, marries Mumtaz Mahal, whose death in childbirth bearing their fourteenth child in 1631 inspired him to build the Taj Mahal in her honor. He started the Taj Mahal shortly after her death and completed it in 1652. The Shah and his wife were together on a military campaign at the time of her death.

Also in 1612, the English translation of the first half of *Don Quixote* by Spanish novelist Cervantes is published.

Chapter 7

THE MOST IMPORTANT WOMAN IN COLONIAL AMERICA

CAPTAIN ARGALL GOES TO THE POTOWOMAC INDIAN VILLAGE

In early April 1613, Captain Samuel Argall goes on a trading mission to the Potowomac village. Unknown to him, this is the village where Princess Pocahontas, her husband Kocoum, and their child Little Kocoum, live. It has been at least four years since Princess Pocahontas has had any interaction with the English settlers. She is 15 years old, having been born September 17, 1597.

ARGALL DISCOVERS THAT POCAHONTAS LIVES IN POTOWOMAC

Chief Japazaw of the Potowomac village is Kocoum's older brother. By chance, Captain Argall learns that Pocahontas lives in the village. He threatens Chief Japazaw and his wife and gets them to bring Pocahontas to lunch on his ship.

CAPTAIN ARGALL KIDNAPS POCAHONTAS

Captain Argall gives Chief Japazaw and his wife a copper kettle and prevents Pocahontas from leaving the ship, kidnapping her. Captain Argall sends soldiers to the village to kill Kocoum, and they are successful. Little

Kocoum is saved by the women of the village and hidden in the forest.

Little Kocoum will have many descendents, including the famous American entertainer Wayne Newton.

CAPTAIN ARGALL HOLDS POCAHONTAS FOR RANSOM

Knowing Pocahontas to be a princess, Captain Argall asks for ransom. He asks for the release of English prisoners held by paramount Chief Powhatan, Pocahontas' father, and return of all English weapons that were acquired by the Indians over the years. Chief Japazaw sends messengers to Chief Powhatan. Two days later the messengers return and report that Chief Powhatan accepts the ransom terms and asks Captain Argall to sail his ship up the Pamunkey River to the village of Matchut to receive the ransom.

AFTER CHIEF POWHATAN AGREES TO THE RANSOM DEMANDS, CAPTAIN ARGALL KEEPS POCAHONTAS PRISONER

On April 13, 1613, after receiving a favorable answer to his ransom demands, Captain Samuel Argall leaves Potowomac, but sails to Jamestown rather than to meet Chief Powhatan and receive the ransom. After reaching Jamestown, Princess Pocahontas is sent to the new village of Henrico, 55 miles upriver from Jamestown. Sir Thomas Dale, the Marshal, is headquartered in Henrico.

CONVERTING POCAHONTAS TO CHRISTIANITY

Pocahontas is sent to the home of Reverend Alexander Whitaker, who along with Governor Dale is a devout Calvinist or Puritan, not an Anglican, to be instructed in Christianity. Reverend Whitaker has a church and about 100 acres fenced off with a parsonage called Rock Hall in Henrico. He serves the churches in both Henrico and another settlement called Bermuda Hundred.

John Rolfe, a widower since his wife died three years earlier in 1610, assists Reverend Whitaker with Pocahontas' Christianity lessons.

JOHN ROLFE WITH HIS CROSS BRED TOBACCO IS THE FINANCIAL SAVIOR OF VIRGINIA

In June 1613, John Rolfe ships samples of his West Indian tobacco to England on the *Elizabeth*. This is his cross bred Trinidad and Orinoco tobacco. Later in the year, Rolfe receives word that his tobacco is compared favorably with the best Spanish leaf, and its price is only slightly below the price for the Spanish tobacco. Rolfe calls his tobacco Orinoco Tobacco. This is Rolfe's second successful crop, and now that it is well received in England he can plant a much larger crop for export the next year.

John Rolfe and his tobacco is recognized as the financial savior of the colony! It has only been a little over four years since Rolfe left England.

SIR THOMAS DALE IN CHARGE AGAIN

The next spring, in March 1614, Sir Thomas Gates returns to England and leaves Sir Thomas Dale in command.

JOHN ROLFE FALLS IN LOVE WITH ... POCAHONTAS!

Over time, during the time they spend together on Christianity lessons, John Rolfe falls in love with Pocahontas and she with him. Rolfe would like to marry Pocahontas, but there is a big problem. At that time, interracial marriage is, at the very least, frowned upon and, as a practical matter, prohibited. Of course there are many colonists living with native women, but they are not married. What is an English gentleman to do?

ROLFE SEEKS TO MARRY POCAHONTAS AND ASKS FOR GOVERNOR DALE'S CONSENT TO THE INTERRACIAL MARRIAGE

John Rolfe writes a very long letter to the colony's Governor, Sir Thomas Dale. He professes his love, not lust, for Pocahontas, and asks for permission to marry her. The text of his long and flowery prose letter, full of Christian fervor and much soul searching, survives. Rolfe recognizes the impediment of interracial marriage and argues that it would be good for all. Pocahontas would become a Christian and live in English society, while the colony would benefit by converting a pagan and having better relations with the natives. Plus he loves her very much.

Ralph Hamor summarizes Rolfe's situation in a simpler style:

Long before this time, a gentleman of approved behavior and honest carriage, Master John Rolfe, had been in love with Pocahontas and she with him ... made known to Sir Thomas Dale by a letter from him [Rolfe], whereby he entreated his advice and furtherance in his life, if so it seemed fit to him [Dale] for the good of the plantation. And Pocahontas herself acquainted her brethren [her brothers] therewith.

In spring 1614, Governor Dale consents to the marriage. Now Rolfe seeks Chief Powhatan's consent to Rolfe's marriage to Powhatan's daughter.

ROLFE SEEKS CHIEF POWHATAN'S CONSENT TO MARRY POCAHONTAS

Governor Dale sends Captain Samuel Argall and 150 men aboard the *Treasurer* up the York River seeking the Indians. In order to show a peaceful intent, John Rolfe and Pocahontas are on board. Captain Samuel Argall is again part of the Pocahontas and John Rolfe story. Captain Argall and his men meet some resistance at the first Indian village they encounter, so they sack and burn the village and kill five or six Indian men.

Farther upriver, at Werowocomoco, which in the early days of Jamestown had been paramount Chief Powhatan's village, the English go ashore with Pocahontas. She refuses to speak to any Indians other than royalty, and two of her brothers come to speak with her. Pocahontas' brothers agree to remain as hostages while John Rolfe and young Rob Sparkes seek Powhatan's permission for Rolfe to wed Pocahontas.

Powhatan is three days journey away, so Rolfe meets with Powhatan's younger brother Opechancanough (sometimes Opechankeno). A message is received from Powhatan. Chief Powhatan gives permission for the marriage of Pocahontas and John Rolfe, and Chief Powhatan further suggests a general peace between the natives and the settlers.

ENGAGED TO BE MARRIED

Rolfe is overjoyed, as he and Pocahontas are now formally engaged. Governor Dale quickly accepts Chief Powhatan's offer of peace.

THE BAPTISM OF POCAHONTAS

Pocahontas is baptized as a Christian in early April 1614, by Reverend Alexander Whitaker who, along with John Rolfe, has instructed her in Christian teachings. The baptism probably took place in Whitaker's Henrico Puritan church, but perhaps in the Jamestown Anglican Church. The baptism is attended by John Rolfe, Governor Dale, and some of Pocahontas' Indian relatives. Princess Pocahontas, who already has adopted English attire, is given the English name of Rebecca.

The Baptism of Pocahontas is commemorated in the United States Capitol building in Washington, D.C. A large painting, 18 feet wide by 12 feet high, of the imagined scene hangs in the rotunda of the building, one of eight similarly sized paintings of the history of the United States. It was commissioned in 1836 and installed in 1840. The painting is a testament to how important the period of peace that followed was to the survival of the colony and the establishment of the United States.

Also, in the 1800's, American settlers on the frontier had a lot of conflict with Indians. In addition, few Indians had been converted to Christianity in over 200 years of trying. Princess Pocahontas' baptism represented the ideal that American government officials had for the way they wanted Indians to behave.

The event was further commemorated in 1870 when an engraving of the Baptism of Pocahontas painting appeared on the back of a $20 bill.

THE MARRIAGE OF POCAHONTAS AND JOHN ROLFE

Shortly after her baptism, on April 5, 1614, Reverend Richard Bucke marries Princess Pocahontas and John Rolfe in the Anglican Church in Jamestown. John Rolfe is a 28 year old widower, and Pocahontas a 16 year old widow. Pocahontas' sister, Mattachanna, her husband the priest Uttamattamakin, and other Indians attend and witness the marriage.

In the summer of 2010, almost 400 years later, archeologists have finally located the foundation of the Jamestown church the Rolfes were married in, which was built in 1608. It was the second church built in Jamestown, as the first church had burned down along with everything else on January 7, 1608. Then in the summer of 2011, archeologists finished excavating the entire footprint of the 1608 church and were surprised at how large it was, 64 feet by 24 feet. This is larger than the later 20 feet by 50 feet brick church which has now been reconstructed. It was much larger than any other building, and would have dominated the 1.1 acre fort.

THE FIRST INTERRACIAL CHURCH MARRIAGE IN THE AMERICAS

John Rolfe and Pocahontas celebrate the first interracial church marriage in America! The Rolfes start married life by living on Hog Island across the river from Jamestown although some sources say they also lived on his Varina Farms plantation.

MEANWHILE, ELSEWHERE, THIS IS HAPPENING ...

In February 1613, sixteen year old Michael Romanov, son of the Patriarch of Moscow, is elected Russian Tsar and founds the Romanov dynasty which then rules Russia from 1613 to 1917, over 300 years.

On June 29, 1613, fire destroys the Globe Theater in London during a performance of William Shakespeare's *Henry VIII* when a canon used for special effects ignites the theater's roof. It burns to the ground.

Chapter 8

JOHN ROLFE'S MARRIAGE SAVES THE COLONY

THE PEACE OF POCAHONTAS

The Peace of Pocahontas begins. It lasts for eight years until 1622. This Peace of Pocahontas is extremely important to the history of America. The colony now has a cash crop, tobacco, thanks to John Rolfe, to enable it to prosper financially. Yet, due to the effects of disease and Indian attack, the colony has been unable to keep enough settlers alive to assure the colony's viability.

This period of peace allows many more settlers to survive, and allows many more settlers to arrive from England, to establish a critical mass of colonists in Virginia so that the Indians can't force them out if the peace ends.

John Rolfe has yet to learn the value to his tobacco crop of his marriage to Pocahontas. For Rolfe it is a love match. It is also an extremely important strategic alliance for the Virginia colony since it was the reason for the Peace of Pocahontas. And Rolfe's marriage alliance would prove extremely important for his tobacco.

THE MOST MOMENTOUS EVENT OF THE 17TH CENTURY?

Rolfe's tobacco this year proved even more successful than the previous year. It was John Rolfe's third successful harvest and his first large export shipment to England. The tobacco shipment sailed on the *Treasurer* on June 28, 1614, commanded by Captain Samuel Argall, the same man who kidnapped Princess Pocahontas the previous year.

The shipment in 1614 of Rolfe's tobacco to London and its sale there has been described by at least one historian as the most momentous event of the 17th century. It is the seed that led to the success of England in America and the eventual world dominance of what would become the United States of America.

ROLFE IS MENTORED BY FORMER ENEMIES

Now that peace prevails and John Rolfe is part of the family, Indians, probably Uttamattamakin (sometimes Tomocomo), who is married to Pocahontas' oldest sister Mattachanna, and other priests who are in charge of curing the Indian tobacco, teach Rolfe how they cure tobacco. They hang individual tobacco leaves up to dry under cover from the weather, rather than pile them under hay to ferment. This change in curing method in 1614 with help from his Indian friends results in John Rolfe producing exceptionally fine tobacco.

John Rolfe probably wasn't even looking for a mentor, as he was the most experienced farmer among the English, and the only one with knowledge of tobacco. Yet Rolfe found a mentor in a very unexpected place, from among his former enemies. It would have required a giant leap of faith for an Englishman to listen to an

Indian mentor since most Englishmen considered the Indians to be savages. The Indian method of curing tobacco was radically different from the traditional English method. John Rolfe embraced this radical new idea and produced a superior tobacco leaf product.

JOHN ROLFE IS APPOINTED SECRETARY OF THE VIRGINIA COLONY

In June 1614, Ralph Hamor, who has been Secretary of the colony since the departure of William Strachey on August 20, 1611, leaves for England. John Rolfe is appointed Secretary of the colony. For this he receives a salary and unspecified privileges.

A SON, THOMAS ROLFE, IS BORN TO JOHN ROLFE AND POCAHONTAS

On January 30, 1615, a son is born to Pocahontas and John Rolfe, and they call him Thomas Rolfe.

PROSPERITY

In 1615, the quantity of tobacco exported to England is 2,000 pounds. A cured tobacco leaf is very light in weight, so that's a lot of tobacco. This means the beginning of true prosperity for Rolfe and the colony. His tobacco is extremely successful in England.

AMERICA'S FIRST ENTREPRENEUR AND THE MOST IMPORTANT WOMAN IN COLONIAL AMERICA ARE INVITED TO GO ON A PROMOTIONAL TOUR TO ENGLAND

In 1616, Governor Sir Thomas Dale asks John Rolfe and his wife to accompany him to London to help promote the colony and its tobacco crop. Even 400 years ago people did promotional tours! Given the tempest, shipwreck, and being marooned on a deserted island experience of Rolfe's only other ocean crossing, it's a wonder he agreed to cross the Atlantic Ocean twice, to England and back to Virginia. He must have been very brave.

The John Rolfe and Pocahontas promotional tour to England shows that even 400 years ago people appreciated that marketing is important. While we can't all market the same way, that is we can't all marry a princess, we can all market our product.

IN JUST SEVEN YEARS, JOHN ROLFE HAS CHANGED THE WORLD

It has now been seven years since John Rolfe stepped onto the *Sea Venture* and into his entrepreneurial adventure. In just seven years John Rolfe has changed the world. The English are now successful in America both financially, thanks to Rolfe's tobacco, and in colonizing, thanks to Rolfe's marriage and the Peace of Pocahontas.

THE UNITED STATES IS ENGLISH SPEAKING AND OF ENGLISH HERITAGE

As a result, the territory that eventually becomes the United States of America now becomes a successful English colony, not a French, Spanish, or Dutch colony. So we have an English heritage and language for the United States. Also, Rolfe founds an industry that will provide America's biggest export for the next 150 years, and will be a multi-billion dollar industry 400 years later.

Of course John Rolfe doesn't live long enough to see all these effects of his entrepreneurial efforts. He even may not realize his actions have changed the world. Rolfe is just a farmer with a strong goal which he has achieved and he is in love, but he does have reason to feel very successful.

JOHN ROLFE SHARES HIS GOOD FORTUNE

Rolfe is personally generous, sharing his good fortune with all the colonists, who also plant his cross bred tobacco. In today's terms, he is giving back to his community.

Rolfe's personal financial rewards are primarily grants of land and, of course, the profits from the sale of his tobacco. It's noteworthy that he shares his seeds and his curing process so everyone thrives. Even front yards in Jamestown are planted with tobacco.

On the light side, John Rolfe is an example of the adage, Good Guys Finish First.

MEANWHILE, ELSEWHERE, THIS IS HAPPENING ...

On April 7, 1614, the Greek/Spanish painter El Greco dies.

Chapter 9

SUCCESSFUL PROMOTIONAL TOUR

TO ENGLAND WITH CAPTAIN ARGALL

In April 1616, John Rolfe, Pocahontas, their 14 month old son Thomas Rolfe, about a dozen Indians, and Sir Thomas Dale, sail aboard the *Treasurer* to England. The ship's captain is Captain Samuel Argall. Pocahontas's oldest sister Mattachanna and her husband the priest Uttamattamakin are two of those who accompany her. Also on board are 2,500 pounds of tobacco, about half of the amount exported to England in 1616.

The *Treasurer* is the same ship and Captain Argall is the same Captain who kidnapped Pocahontas in April 1613.

SPANISH PRISONERS

Also on board the *Treasurer* are two Spanish prisoners, Captain Don Diego de Molina and his pilot Francis Lembry, who were captured in May 1611, nearly five years before. During the voyage, Lembry is discovered to be an Englishman working for the Spanish, and he is hanged as a traitor somewhere in the middle of the Atlantic.

ARRIVAL IN ENGLAND
On June 3, 1616, the *Treasurer* docks at Plymouth, England, over 200 miles from London. The Rolfes travel by coach on the coach road to London.

On June 12, 1616, Pocahontas, John Rolfe, and their son Thomas Rolfe reach London. Pocahontas' sister Mattachanna and her sister's husband the priest Uttamattamakin and ten other natives accompany them.

HIGH SOCIETY
Sir Edwin Sandys, a Member of Parliament and a rising star in the Virginia Company of London, helps John and Rebecca Rolfe in London. They are invited and entertained by many titled and high society people.

THE FAMOUS SIMON VAN DE PASSE PORTRAIT
Later that year, Simon Van de Passe, a well-known engraver, is commissioned to engrave a portrait of Pocahontas and she sits for the portrait. Engravings of her sell all over London and cause a popular sensation. Pocahontas is a celebrity!

AUDIENCE WITH THE QUEEN
In the fall of 1616, the Rolfes have an audience with Queen Anne. The couple and their Indian companions are celebrated throughout English society. Rolfe's success with tobacco is only exceeded by his wife's popularity.

TWELFTH NIGHT WITH KING JAMES I AND QUEEN ANNE
On January 6, 1617, the Rolfes attend the Twelfth Night masque given by King James I as guests of Queen

Anne and the King. The play presented at the event is written by Ben Jonson and called *The Vision of Delight*. It is quite an honor for gentleman John Rolfe, successful entrepreneur, but not a noble, to be invited and to meet the King.

REPORT TO THE KING

While in London, John Rolfe writes a long report "To the King's Most Sacred Majesty" titled *"A True Relation of the State of Virginia When Left by Sir Thomas Dale, Knight, in May Last, 1616."* He reports to King James I that there are 351 residents in Virginia, in which of the various residential areas they live, enumerates the cattle, horses, goats, hogs, and poultry, details the many different crops grown, and cites the fish, fowl, and deer available to catch. Rolfe's religious fervor in this report, while still present, is somewhat less than it was in his letter to Sir Thomas Dale seeking permission to marry outside his race.

It's an honor for gentleman farmer John Rolfe to write directly to the King, even if it is in his capacity of Secretary of the Virginia colony.

LONDON'S FOUL AIR

Understandably, Pocahontas and her Indian companions who have lived their whole lives in the clean forest air of Virginia don't like the thick coal smoke which fouls London's air. So, in February 1617, the Rolfes move from London to Brentford, a village about 9 miles north of London on the Thames River, where the air is cleaner.

SMITH IS ALIVE

During Pocahontas' visit to England, she, then Rebecca Rolfe, sees John Smith on one occasion and is surprised that he is alive, as her people had been told he died from his burns in 1609. She had last seen him in 1608 when she was 10 and 11 years old.

RETURNING TO VIRGINIA

The Rolfes decide it's time to go home to Virginia. In March 1617, John Rolfe, Pocahontas, and the Indian party board the *Treasurer*, the same ship that brought them to England and also the same ship used in kidnapping Pocahontas, whose captain is Captain Samuel Argall, the same captain who brought them to England and who kidnapped Pocahontas in 1613. They sail down the Thames River heading for Jamestown. Argall is in command of a three ship fleet, including the *George*.

POCAHONTAS, REBECCA ROLFE, PASSES ON

On March 21, 1617, Pocahontas takes ill on board ship on the way down the Thames River. They stop in Gravesend and take her to an inn, and Pocahontas dies in the inn at Gravesend, Kent, England, 25 miles downstream from London. Pocahontas, born September 17, 1597 and died March 21, 1617, is not yet 20 years old. She is survived by two children, Little Kocoum and Thomas Rolfe. They will provide her with thousands of descendants.

John Rolfe and Captain Argall and the *George* stay in Gravesend for Pocahontas' funeral which is held in St. George's Church, Gravesend, England. Pocahontas is buried in the vault beneath the chancel of the church. John Rolfe is once again a widower.

Meanwhile, the *Treasurer* goes ahead to Plymouth, England, for final provisioning.

POISON?

The Mattaponi tribe of the Powhatan nation tells the story of Pocahontas' death differently. Their "sacred oral history" is that John Rolfe and Pocahontas are having dinner with Captain Samuel Argall in the Captain's cabin of the *Treasurer* on the first night of the voyage and Pocahontas becomes ill. When she returns to her quarters, she feels sick in her stomach and vomits. Pocahontas tells her sister Mattachanna and brother-in-law Uttamattamakin that she thinks the English must have put something in her food. She begins to convulse, and Mattachanna goes and gets John Rolfe. By the time they return to Pocahontas's quarters, she is dead. Back in Virginia, Mattachanna and Uttamattamakin tell Chief Powhatan Wahunsenaca that Pocahontas was murdered in England, most likely poisoned.

TWO YEAR OLD THOMAS ROLFE STAYS IN ENGLAND

When John Rolfe arrives in Plymouth, about 170 miles from Gravesend, with Captain Argall on the *George*, his son Thomas Rolfe is seriously ill. Thomas is just over two years old. Rolfe is afraid the ocean voyage to Virginia will be too much for Thomas and could kill him. So, John Rolfe leaves his son Thomas Rolfe with Sir Louis Stukely, the vice admiral for Devonshire, and arranges for Stukely to care for Thomas until John Rolfe's younger brother Henry Rolfe can come from London to get him. Now he must leave his little son, having just lost his beloved wife. Henry Rolfe takes care of and raises Thomas Rolfe.

BACK IN VIRGINIA

Having yet endured another personal tragedy, John Rolfe experiences a successful voyage which involves a short passage of only 35 days and the death of only one man at sea. Captain Samuel Argall and John Rolfe reach Jamestown on May 16, 1617. Much has changed in the few short years since passage was expected to take almost four months.

Rolfe learns that Reverend Alexander Whitaker has drowned in one of the rivers in early 1617 while Rolfe was in England. During the summer of 1617, a smallpox epidemic breaks out in Virginia.

CHIEF POWHATAN RESIGNS AS PARAMOUNT CHIEF

Pocahontas' father Wahunsenaca, known as Chief Powhatan, turns over his position as paramount chief to his younger brother Opechancanough, who is chief of the Pamunkey tribe, bypassing another brother Opitchapam who is older but considered weak and lacking in leadership ability. The new paramount chief Opechancanough has a reputation as a warrior.

THE VIRGINIA COLONY IS VERY, VERY PROFITABLE

Exports of tobacco to England in 1617 total 20,000 pounds (one source, Wikipedia, says 50,000 pounds). This makes the colony's fortune. The English are in Virginia to stay.

THE SPANISH MONOPOLY OVER TOBACCO IS BROKEN

In June 1618, The *George* carries 20,000 pounds of tobacco to England. Total exports of tobacco to

England in 1618 are 40,000 pounds. The Spanish monopoly is broken.

MEANWHILE, ELSEWHERE, THIS IS HAPPENING ...

On April 23, 1616, while the Rolfes sail to England, William Shakespeare dies. It is his 52nd birthday. Shakespeare and England are still using the Julian calendar at this time. Shakespeare was born on April 23, 1564 and baptized on April 26, 1564. He married Anne Hathaway on November 27, 1582.

Spanish novelist, poet, and playwright, Miguel Cervantes, author of the first modern novel *Don Quixote* also dies on April 23, 1616, by the Gregorian calendar, which is the calendar we use today and which most of Europe used then. Cervantes was baptized October 9, 1547. Thus Cervantes dies on the same date as Shakespeare, although not the same day because of the different calendars used.

On November 25, 1616, Cardinal Richelieu, at that time still a Bishop, joins the French Government for the first time as Secretary of State under King Louis XIII.

Chapter 10

PILLAR OF THE COMMUNITY

JOHN ROLFE MARRIES JANE PIERCE

After returning to Virginia, John Rolfe marries Jane Pierce, a widow and the daughter of William and Joan Pierce. William Pierce came to Virginia and was shipwrecked on the *Sea Venture* with Rolfe. Jane Pierce, who was 10 years old at the time, and her mother Joan, came to Virginia in 1609 on the *Blessing*, part of the fleet that included the *Sea Venture*. They survived the Starving Time and were reunited with William when the *Sea Venture* survivors arrived in 1610. This is John Rolfe's third marriage. Jane Pierce is one of the few people who know all that John Rolfe has been through.

John Rolfe continues planting tobacco and is recognized as a pillar of the community. I trust Rolfe is enjoying his success and I hope that he celebrates his success.

POCAHONTAS' FATHER DIES

In April 1618, Wahunsenaca, formerly Chief Powhatan dies at age 78 (1540 to April 1618) within a year of Pocahontas's death. Some sources put his death in 1622, and some sources say he was almost 90 years old, putting his birth some years earlier in 1535.

THE PEACE OF POCAHONTAS ENCOURAGES SETTLORS

In the next three years, from 1618 to 1621, the Virginia Company of London sends 50 ships and almost 4,000 men and women to Virginia as settlers. This compares with just 1,600 settlers sent to Virginia in the nine years from 1607 to 1616.

JOHN ROLFE IS A MEMBER OF THE FIRST LEGISLATIVE ASSEMBLY ON AMERICAN SOIL

John Rolfe, already Secretary of the colony since June 1614, is appointed as one of the initial members of the first legislative assembly on American soil, the House of Burgesses, which meets for the first time in Jamestown on July 30, 1619. The group is composed of Governor George Yeardley, six councilors including John Rolfe, and two representatives from each of the small settlements in the Tidewater region. They meet in the choir of the church in Jamestown, the third church, which has been reconstructed and can be visited in Historic Jamestown.

Thus begins the form of representative government that will later evolve to shape the government of the United States of America.

JOHN ROLFE IS A FATHER AGAIN

John Rolfe and Jane Pierce Rolfe welcome a daughter named Elizabeth Rolfe in 1620.

In 1620, tobacco exports to England are over 40,000 pounds.

THE VIRGINIA COMPANY OF LONDON'S COLONIAL COUNCIL

In 1621, John Rolfe is named to the Colonial Council which is selected by the Virginia Company of London's London officers and which conducts most of the colony's business. Sir Edwin Sandys is Treasurer of the Company.

JOHN ROLFE IS ILL AND WRITES HIS WILL

On March 10, 1622, a Sunday, John Rolfe is ill and dictates his Will to Reverend Richard Bucke who transcribes it. Rolfe signs his Will and it is witnessed by Reverend Bucke. He leaves property to his son Thomas Rolfe and to his wife Jane and daughter Elizabeth Rolfe. John Rolfe has not seen his son Thomas since leaving him in England when Thomas was too ill to attempt the ocean crossing, and never sees him again.

THE PEACE OF POCAHONTAS ENDS

On Friday, March 22, 1622, five years and a day after Pocahontas' death, Indians massacre 347 colonists and burn Henrico. The colonists in and around Jamestown, including the John Rolfe family, are safe, although some Indian sources suggest John Rolfe may have been killed on this day. This is the end of the Peace of Pocahontas.

Chief Opechancanough is responsible for the massacre. He decides it is time to rid Virginia of the English. It turns out to be too late to do that. The Peace of Pocahontas enabled the English to get enough colonists in Virginia to withstand even this massacre.

JOHN ROLFE PASSES ON

In April 1622, John Rolfe dies, most sources say, in Virginia. One source says he dies while a passenger on the *Neptune* bound for England. He is 36 years old, about a month short of his 37th birthday on May 6.

Later in 1622, John Rolfe's widow Joan Rolfe marries Captain Roger Smith. Elizabeth Rolfe, daughter of Joan and John Rolfe, is raised in the Joan and Roger Smith household.

THOMAS ROLFE COMES TO VIRGINIA TO RECEIVE HIS LEGACY

Reportedly the English continually seek more land from the Powhatan Indians. Chief Opechancanough steadfastly replies that they will not give any more land except to Pocahontas' son, Thomas Rolfe.

Thomas Rolfe comes to Virginia in 1635 to claim his inheritance. He is 20 years old. Aside from taking possession of the land his father John Rolfe left him, Thomas Rolfe visits Chief Opechancanough and his Indian relatives and receives a large tract of land that was set aside for him by Chief Powhatan because he is Pocahontas' son.

MEANWHILE, ELSEWHERE, THIS IS HAPPENING …

In England, on June 7, 1618, Sir Thomas West, Lord De La Warr dies.

Sir Walter Raleigh is beheaded on October 29, 1618 for conspiring against King James I. His last request before being executed is for a smoke. His request is granted and a tradition for the condemned is born.

On August 19, 1619, Sir Thomas Dale dies in England.

Thirty-eight colonists from Berkeley Parish in England disembark in Virginia on December 4, 1619 and give thanks to God. This is sometimes considered the first Thanksgiving in the Americas.

On September 6, 1620, the *Mayflower* leaves Plymouth England and lands at Cape Cod on November 11, 1620 with Pilgrims and Planters. The Mayflower Compact is signed. In December 1620, the *Mayflower* and the Pilgrims land at Plymouth Rock in Plymouth, Massachusetts.

On February 28, 1621, Cosimo II de Medici, Grand Duke of Tuscany, dies in Florence of tuberculosis. He was born May 12, 1590 and reigned from February

17, 1609 to his death at age 30 on February 28, 1621. As a child he was tutored by Galileo Galilei and is best remembered as Galileo's patron.

In October 1621, the Pilgrims of Plymouth Colony celebrate a three day harvest festival with the Wampanoag Indians, often considered the first Thanksgiving. It was actually a victory celebration because the Pilgrims had used their weapons to kill the Indian enemies of the Wampanoag Indians in exchange for learning how to plant and harvest corn and other crops.

On May 24, 1624, King James I revokes the Charter of the Virginia Company of London and the Virginia Company of London dissolves. Virginia becomes a Royal Colony. Jamestown is the capital of the Royal Colony of Virginia through 1698. In 1699, the capital is moved to Middle Plantation, now called Williamsburg.

King James I dies on March 27, 1625. His son King Charles I is his successor.

Chief Opechancanough tries one more time to force the English out of Virginia, on April 18, 1644. He chooses this time because he has heard of the civil war in England which a few years later led to the execution of King Charles I. In a coordinated attack, the Indians kill 400-500 of the 8,000 settlers in Virginia. After two years of skirmishes, Opechancanough is captured in March 1646 and held in a prison cell in Jamestown. Opechancanough is reportedly nearly 100 years old. He is virtually blind and needs assistants to hold his eyelids open. Opechancanough cannot walk without assistance and is so frail that he is usually carried on a litter. After about two weeks of imprisonment in Jamestown, Opechancanough is murdered in his cell by a vengeful jailer who shoots Opechancanough in the back.

In 1646, the Powhatan Indians and the English sign a peace treaty and the Indians are removed to a small reservation.

In 1958, the wreck of the *Sea Venture* is discovered by Bermudian diver Edmund Downing. In 1992, the *Sea Venture* excavation is completed and surviving artifacts retrieved.

EPILOGUE

John Rolfe certainly did meet the dictionary definition of an entrepreneur: "a person who organizes and manages any enterprise, especially a business, usually with considerable initiative and risk." He used lots of initiative, organized, and managed his business, and he faced an outrageous amount of risk.

Rolfe was able to create his vision, have freedom to life his life as he wanted, earn lots of money, and leave a tremendous legacy to his family and to all Americans.

John Rolfe had an entrepreneurial vision of growing, harvesting, and curing mild Caribbean tobacco in Virginia and exporting it to England. He made a committed decision and took his wife to Virginia to settle and make his vision a reality. He got the money required for his enterprise. He had a business plan. He knew there would be risks, and he accepted and even embraced them. Then there were the unexpected obstacles and setbacks. He dealt with those and continued on with getting to his goal. He endured several tragedies in his personal life and still continued. When his tobacco leaf was pronounced very good he still kept improving it. He remarried and secured an alliance which he probably wasn't expecting. He took a radical new idea and advice from a former enemy who became his mentor. This contributed directly to his tremendous success. He embarked on a promotional tour to England that made his wife a celebrity and him and his tobacco second fiddle. But it all helped promote his Orinoco Tobacco. He had succeeded and was respected by his fellow colonists and had an audience with the King and Queen of England. He also shared his success with his fellow settlers.

The Virginia colony was failing financially and the London investors were about to pull the plug. John Rolfe's cash crop saved Virginia and the English colonial effort in America.

Yet, the Virginia colony was still not on a sound footing politically because of the Indian war. The colonists were being killed off and there weren't enough of them. John Rolfe's love for and marriage to Princess Pocahontas changed all that. Their marriage started the Peace of Pocahontas which allowed the political success of the English in America.

John Rolfe and Pocahontas' marriage was a milestone because it was the first interracial church marriage in the Americas.

With the success of the English colony in Virginia, the stage was set for English colonies elsewhere, such as in Massachusetts. And even though the French, Spanish, and Dutch had an earlier presence in North America, the area which became the United States ended up with an English heritage, English common law, and the English language. It could have been very different but for John Rolfe's cash crop and John Rolfe's marriage to Pocahontas.

In seven years, John Rolfe achieved much more than he had planned. His entrepreneurial initiative and courage had changed the world.

HISTORICAL CONTEXT

The action in John Rolfe's story begins in 1609. Yet much happened in the 100 years before that date which bears on his story. This Historical Context is a brief summary of important events that shaped what happened in 1609 and beyond.

CHRISTOPHER COLUMBUS DISCOVERS THE AMERICAS

On October 12, 1492, Christopher Columbus, sailing for the Spanish King Ferdinand II and Queen Isabella I, discovers the Americas for Spain, lands on Hispaniola which is present day Dominican Republic in the Caribbean, and establishes a settlement there. Columbus sails west across the Atlantic Ocean from Spain in the hopes of reaching Asia to establish a new route for trading spices. The old route for trading with Asia by going through the eastern Mediterranean area was closed to Europeans in 1453 when Muslims captured Constantinople. Now, instead of finding a new trade route, Columbus and the Spanish focus on finding wealth in the Americas. The Portuguese, French, and Dutch do the same. England gets a slow start.

DISCOVERY OF BERMUDA

In 1503, Juan de Bermudez discovers the islands later called Bermuda, but he can't set foot on the islands because of the reefs surrounding them. He returns in

1515 to land hogs on the islands so that passing Spanish ships can replenish their stores. Again he can't land because of the reefs, but he throws hogs overboard and they swim ashore.

MARTIN LUTHER: PROTESTANT

Martin Luther presents his 95 Theses in Wittenberg, Germany, on October 31, 1517, All Saints' Eve. They are translated from Latin to German, printed on a printing press, and widely disseminated in January 1518. This is the beginning of the Protestant religious movement.

SPAIN CONQUERS CENTRAL AMERICA AND PERU

Hernán Cortés conquers the Aztecs in Mexico in 1521. Francisco Pizarro begins subjugation of the Incas in Peru in 1533. These two colonies and their gold and silver give Spain immense wealth and power in the world.

FRENCH EXPLORERS VERRAZZANO AND CARTIER IN AMERICA

In 1524, Giovanni da Verrazzano, a Venetian sailing for France, explores the American coast from the Bahamas to Nova Scotia. Verrazzano claims all the land for France. And in 1534, Jacques Cartier, a Frenchman sailing for France, makes the first of his three voyages to North America, exploring the St. Lawrence River upstream as far as Montreal.

WHALING IN LABRADOR

In 1540, Basque fishermen from Northern Spain set up a whale oil processing plant on Labrador, in what is now Canada.

BIRTH OF WAHUNSENACA, CHIEF POWHATAN

Also in 1540, on June 17, a Pamunkey Indian named Wahunsenaca (sometimes Wahunsonacock) is born. He will later unite approximately 31 Algonquian tribes in the Tidewater area into the Powhatan confederacy and become their paramount chief, Chief Powhatan. Wahunsenaca's first wife is from the Mattaponi tribe and is named Pocahontas. She bears several children to Chief Powhatan, and dies during the birth of her daughter Matoaka, later known as Princess Pocahontas.

BLOODY MARY

On October 1, 1553, Mary Tutor is crowned Queen of England at age 37. She is the daughter of King Henry VIII and his first wife, Catherine of Aragon. Queen Mary is Catholic like her mother, and like her father King Henry VIII was until he annulled his marriage to Catherine of Aragon. Ironically, King Henry VIII was awarded the title "Defender of the Faith" by Pope Leo X on October 11, 1521, for his treatise attacking Lutheranism. Queen Mary succeeds her half brother King Edward VI, who is the son of King Henry VIII and his third wife, Jane Seymour, and King Henry VIII's only male heir. Jane Seymour dies 12 days after the birth of Edward of an infection.

Queen Mary is known as Bloody Mary for killing over 300 Protestants by burning them alive. On July 25, 1554, Queen Mary marries the Spanish Catholic heir, and he becomes King Philip II of Spain in 1556. Queen Mary dies of stomach cancer on November 17, 1558, after a reign of only five years.

THE ELIZABETHAN AGE

Elizabeth I is crowned Queen of England on January 15, 1559, succeeding Queen "Bloody" Mary. Elizabeth is 25 years old and the only child of King Henry VIII and his second wife Queen Consort Anne Boleyn, who is famously beheaded when Princess Elizabeth is two years old. Queen Elizabeth rules for 44 years until her death in 1603 at age 67. Her reign is now known as the Elizabethan Age.

Catholic King Philip II of Spain, now a widower, regards Queen Elizabeth as illegitimate and a heretic. He supports plots to overthrow Queen Elizabeth in favor of her Catholic cousin Mary Queen of Scots. Mary Queen of Scots is executed in 1587 by Queen Elizabeth.

KIDNAPPED INDIAN CALLED DON LUIS DE VELASCO

In 1561, a Spanish fleet off what is now North Carolina seizes a young Indian boy and takes him to Spain. From Spain he is sent to Mexico and educated by Dominican Friars among the conquered Aztecs. He is given the name Don Luis de Velasco. Later he is sent to Havana, and then in 1566 to Spain again. In 1570, Don Luis goes back to Havana, and then is returned home. Most historians say Don Luis is a cousin of future Chief Powhatan.

WILLIAM SHAKESPEARE

Five years into Elizabeth's reign, on April 23, 1564, William Shakespeare, perhaps the most famous person in the history of Western literature, is born in England.

FRENCH SETTLEMENT IN FLORIDA

In 1565, French Protestants settle at La Caroline on the St. James River in Florida. They only last a few months because the Spanish attack and slaughter them as heretics.

SPANISH ESTABLISH FIRST PERMANENT EUROPEAN SETTLEMENT IN WHAT WOULD BECOME THE UNITED STATES AT ST. AUGUSTINE

On August 28, 1565, on the feast day of St. Augustine of Hippo, Spanish explorers sight land and subsequently disembark on September 7, 1565, at a place they name St. Augustine, in what is now Florida. This is the first permanent European settlement in what will become the United States.

Three years later, in 1568, Spanish missions are established in what is now the state of Georgia, but they don't last.

SPAIN ANNEXES PORTUGAL

In 1580, Spain becomes even more powerful when it essentially annexes Portugal, as King Philip II of Spain also becomes King Philip I of Portugal, and creates a huge global empire.

THE GREGORIAN CALENDAR REPLACES THE JULIAN CALENDAR

The Julian calendar was promulgated in 45 B.C.E. by Roman Emperor Julius Caesar. It has a year of 365 days with a leap year every fourth year. It is fairly accurate when judged by the equinox times which start the seasons of spring and fall. However, it is actually 11 minutes too long. Over long periods of time, the Julian calendar gains about three days every 400 years, or one day every 134 years, when compared with the equinox times.

About 1600 years later, on February 24, 1582, Pope Gregory XIII promulgates the Gregorian calendar to fix the problem. The new calendar is adopted immediately by Europe's Catholic countries. It is another 170 years until England and her colonies, including the Americas, adopt the Gregorian calendar on Thursday, September 14, 1752 (which directly follows Wednesday, September 2, 1752). The Gregorian calendar is finally adopted by Russia in 1918 and Greece in 1923.

MANY COUNTRIES FISHED COD FROM THE GRAND BANKS OFF NEWFOUNDLAND
Dozens of ships from several different European countries fish cod from the Grand Banks off Newfoundland.

FIRST ENGLISH ATTEMPT AT SETTLEMENT IN THE AMERICAS
Although the English are clearly late to the exploration game, their first several attempts at establishing English colonies in North America fail.

Queen Elizabeth I grants a colonizing patent to Sir Humphrey Gilbert, who is a half brother to Walter Raleigh. The first attempt at English settlement in the Americas is by Gilbert with four ships of settlers at St. John's Harbor in Newfoundland, arriving on August 5, 1583. At the time of Gilbert's settlement at St. John's Harbor in Newfoundland there are 36 fishing vessels from various countries at anchor in the harbor. As you can imagine, Gilbert's claiming the land of

Newfoundland for England amused the fishermen from other countries.

The settlers are quickly discouraged, and 17 days after they arrive, they steal a fishing vessel and sail for England. Gilbert dies in a storm off the Azores later that year.

SECOND, THIRD, AND FOURTH ENGLISH ATTEMPTS AT SETTLEMENT IN THE AMERICAS: WALTER RALEIGH AND ROANOKE ISLAND

Walter Raleigh then obtains a royal colonizing patent from Queen Elizabeth I. His 1584 expedition to Roanoke Island in what is now North Carolina leaves colonists and brings some Indian captives back to England. On January 5, 1585, Queen Elizabeth I knights Raleigh, making him Sir Walter Raleigh. He is also made Governor of the American territory and receives the Queen's permission to name the area Virginia in her honor. This is a reference to the fact that Queen Elizabeth has never married and is called The Virgin Queen. The Roanoke Island settlers disappear, and two more attempts at establishing a colony on Roanoke Island fail in 1585 and 1586.

ENGLAND AND SPAIN AT WAR

In May 1585, King Philip II of Spain seizes all English ships in Spanish ports. On August 17, 1585, Catholic Spanish forces capture Antwerp in the Netherlands, and order all Protestants to leave the city. More than half of Antwerp's 100,000 inhabitants go north. On August 20, 1585, Queen Elizabeth signs a treaty committing England to support the Dutch revolt against the Spanish and French Catholic League forces in the Netherlands. The treaty is signed at the Nonsuch Palace in Surrey, England, and is called the Treaty of Nonsuch. King Philip II of Spain takes the signing of the treaty as a declaration of war by Queen Elizabeth against him.

SPANISH ARMADA, 1588

Thirty years earlier, Spanish King Philip II was married to English Queen Mary Tutor, known as Bloody Mary, and he covets the English throne. He plans to invade England and rid it of its Protestant Queen Elizabeth I. He prepares a large invasion fleet of 151 ships and 18,000 soldiers. They are to stop in the Spanish Netherlands near present day Calais, France, to assist a force of 30,000 more troops who are then to join the invasion. They set sail from Lisbon on May 28, 1588.

The Spanish Armada meets the English in the English Channel, and beginning on July 21, 1588, the English fleet and Spanish fleets engage intermittently. The English ships are faster and more maneuverable, they employ better strategy, and the weather assists the English in their utter defeat of the Spanish Armada.

The decisive battle is fought on August 8, 1588, near Gravelines, Flanders. Only 67 of 151 Spanish ships return to Spain, a loss of 84 ships. The English lose no ships and suffer only 50-100 dead and 400 wounded. This is a total victory for the English. The success of the English and the devastating blow to the Spanish fleet is considered a major shift in control of the seas. The 1588 defeat of the Spanish Armada is one of the few dates I remember from high school history.

OTHER FAMOUS PEOPLE OF THE SAME PERIOD

In India, Shah Jahan, the man who built the Taj Mahal, is born on January 5, 1592.

Italian painter Jacopo Tintoretto dies in Venice on May 31, 1594.

William Shakespeare's play *Romeo and Juliet* is first performed on January 29, 1595. Later in 1595, Shakespeare writes *A Midsummer's Night Dream*.

Flemish portrait painter Anthony van Dyke is born on March 22, 1599.

Spanish painter Diego Velázquez is born on June 6, 1599.

PEACE TREATY BETWEEN ENGLAND AND SPAIN

King James I is crowned King of England in 1603, after the death of Queen Elizabeth I, and rules for almost 22 years. King James I and King Philip III of Spain sign a peace treaty in 1604, finally ending the conflict that started in 1585 between their predecessors.

KING JAMES I PUBLISHES A PAMPHLET AGAINST TOBACCO

In 1604, King James I publishes a diatribe called *A Counter-Blast to Tobacco* in which he calls smoking a pipe a filthy habit.

KING JAMES I CHARTERS TWO VIRGINIA COMPANIES

King James I grants a royal charter on April 10, 1606, creating two companies with rights to colonize in North America, the Virginia Company of London and the Virginia Company of Plymouth, named after the English cities in which the principal backers live.

VIRGINIA COMPANY OF PLYMOUTH'S TERRITORY

The Virginia Company of Plymouth has the right to exploit the area from 38 degrees North latitude to 45 degrees North latitude, roughly Delaware Bay north through most of Nova Scotia. The Virginia Company of Plymouth's territory partially overlaps the Virginia Company of London's territory, so the charter provides that any settlement must be 100 miles from the other company's settlement.

POPHAM, OR SAGADAHOC, COLONY FAILS AFTER THE SUCCESS OF JAMESTOWN

The Virginia Company of Plymouth's first attempt at settlement fails. On August 13, 1607, three months after the Virginia Company of London's first adventurers land at Jamestown, settlers are landed from the ship *Gift of God* at the mouth of the Kennebec River and establish the Fort St. George or Popham Colony in Sagadahoc in what is now Maine. Just over a year later, the remaining colonists leave Maine for England on a ship that they build, a 30 ton pinnace called the *Virginia*, which is the first ship built in North America. In 1609, the *Virginia* will play a role in Jamestown history as one of the nine ships in the *Sea Venture* fleet, the rescue attempt known as the Third Supply, sailing to Jamestown, Virginia, from England.

PLYMOUTH COLONY

Thirteen years after the founding of Jamestown, the Virginia Company of London grants a land patent to a group of settlers on a ship called the *Mayflower* to settle at the mouth of the Hudson River. However, the ship goes farther north outside of the lands of the Virginia Company of London and lands in December 1620, in what is now Massachusetts, and calls their colony Plymouth. About 40% of the adults were seeking religious freedom for their Calvinist or Puritan religious practices, with the other 60% of adults seeking profits like the Jamestown venture.

VIRGINIA COMPANY OF LONDON

The men named as receiving the King's grant for the Virginia Company of London are: Sir Thomas Gates, soon to be Governor of the Virginia colony, Sir George Somers, then mayor of Lyme Regis and soon to be Admiral of the Third Supply fleet, who will also sail on the *Sea Venture* and be credited with settling Bermuda, Richard Hakluyt, a geographic expert and publisher and editor of books on exploring the Americas, and Edward Maria Wingfield, who is soon to be elected first President of the Council in Virginia.

The Virginia Company of London has the right to exploit the area from 34 degrees North latitude to 41 degrees North latitude, roughly Cape Fear North Carolina to Long Island Sound. The Virginia Company of London doesn't want to fail as all the others have. They prepare to send the largest group of ships and the largest group of adventurers ever to North America.

1606 VOYAGE TO VIRGINIA

The first group to go to Virginia sails in three ships, the flagship *Susan Constant* commanded by Captain Christopher Newport and carrying a total of 71 people, the *Godspeed* commanded by Captain Bartholomew Gosnold and carrying 52 people, and the *Discovery* commanded by Captain John Ratcliffe. The total of 104 adventurers and 40 crew members leave London on December 20, 1606, and arrive on the Virginia coast on April 26, 1607. They scout for an advantageous site and finally choose the Jamestown site for their fort and settlement. They land on May 14, 1607, almost five months after sailing, and name their settlement after their King.

SMITH SENTENCED TO DEATH ON THE WAY TO JAMESTOWN

Early in the voyage, January 6, 1607, Captain Christopher Newport has one of the passengers of the *Susan Constant*, John Smith, chained in the hold for mutiny. Smith is to be executed in Nevis in the Caribbean, but someone convinces Captain Newport to let him live. Smith remains chained for nearly a month after the ship lands in Virginia.

JOHN SMITH IN JAMESTOWN

John Smith is an important and contentious figure in early Jamestown history, arriving with the first ship, the *Susan Constant*, in 1607, and departing for good on October 4, 1609. He is an inveterate writer and shameless self-promoter, sometimes making up things so he would have a better story. He is a commoner and a lifelong soldier and adventurer, a real soldier of fortune.

When the ships arrive at Jamestown, the leaders of the expedition get together and open the sealed instructions they have from the Virginia Company of London. The instructions name the seven men who will be the governing council, and the seven will elect one to serve as President. The seven are: Captain Christopher Newport, Captain Bartholomew Gosnold, Captain John Ratcliffe, Captain John Martin, Captain George Kendall, Master Edward Maria Wingfield, and John Smith. All are surprised that the commoner John Smith is named as one of the council. Captain Newport refuses to release him and let him join the Council. Edward Maria Wingfield is elected President of the Council.

After the intervention of Reverend Richard Hunt, Captain Newport and Council President Wingfield relent and release Smith on June 10, 1607. They agree to allow Smith to join the Council. On June 14, 1607, Smith joins the Council.

CAPTAIN NEWPORT LEAVES THE ADVENTURERS IN JAMESTOWN

Captain Christopher Newport leaves on June 22, 1607 in the *Susan Constant* along with the *Godspeed* and returns to England. 104 men, and no women, remain in Jamestown with the small ship the *Discovery* which is suitable for exploring the rivers, Chesapeake Bay, and the coast.

In the summer of 1607, the settlers need food. The settlers draw lots to see who will take their new barge and small pinnace and try to trade with the Indians for corn. John Smith has the dubious success of "winning" and takes a few men with him. He goes up the Chickahominy River and meets the Chickahominy tribe which is not a part of the Powhatan Empire. The Chickahominy tribe trades with Smith. He returns to Jamestown a hero. He goes two more times and returns with large amounts of corn.

On August 22, 1607, Council member Bartholomew Gosnold dies. On September 10, 1607, Wingfield is deposed from the Presidency and arrested and Ratcliffe is named President. A short time later, Kendall is tried for conspiracy and executed.

SMITH CAPTURED BY POWHATAN INDIANS

In December 1607, on his fourth trip up the Chickahominy River, John Smith goes past the Chickahominy territory and into joint hunting territory shared with the Powhatan and is captured by Opechancanough, werowance or chief of the Pamunkey tribe and brother to the paramount chief of the Powhatan Empire, Wahunsenaca, known as Chief Powhatan. Two of Smith's men are killed.

Some weeks later, Smith is taken to Werowocomoco on the York River and received by the paramount Chief Powhatan. Pocahontas had just turned 10 years old on September 17, 1607, and was not present. Indian sources are adamant and historians agree, that John Smith was not about to be beaten to death by the Powhatan and was not saved by Pocahontas. As a child, even the child of the chief, she would not have been at the audience of the prisoner. A popular animated film with a disclaimer at the end of the credits (that very few people see) says it is not historically accurate but for entertainment, has given many people a quite different impression of the facts.

SMITH CONVICTED OF MURDER AND SENTENCED TO DEATH, AGAIN

On January 2, 1608, John Smith is returned to Jamestown by the Powhatan tribe. Within hours of his return, Smith is accused by President Ratcliffe of murder for being responsible for the deaths of two of his men at the hands of the Indians when he was captured. Smith is tried, convicted, and sentenced to death with the execution scheduled the next morning.

THE FIRST SUPPLY

Also on January 2, 1608, a Saturday, Captain Christopher Newport returns to Jamestown in the *John and Francis* with the First Supply and 60 settlers. He discovers that only 38 of the 104 settlers alive in June have survived, meaning that 66 settlers have died of disease or Indian attack in just over six months. The second ship of the First Supply, the *Phoenix*, is lost in a fog bank. Captain Newport intervenes in the planned Smith execution.

SMITH PARDONED AGAIN

Only Newport's unexpected arrival and intervention saves Smith from the other colonists led by Gabriel Archer (who later returned as part of the Third Supply as Captain of the *Blessing*), Captain John Ratcliffe (who later returned as part of the Third Supply as Vice Admiral and Captain of the *Diamond*), and John Martin (who later returned as part of the Third Supply as Captain of the *Falcon*), all of whom had arrived in 1607 with Smith, had returned to England, and then came back to Jamestown. Archer and Ratcliffe have served on the colony's council with Smith.

This is the second time John Smith is condemned to death and scheduled for execution by his fellow Englishmen. It is ironic that the man who saved him from death on the second occasion, Captain Christopher Newport, is the same man who condemned him to death on the first occasion!

FIRE

On January 7, 1608, fire rages through Jamestown destroying most of the buildings and supplies, including all the houses, the first Church, and the foodstuffs which have just arrived with the First Supply.

On April 10, 1608, Captain Newport sails to England on the *John and Francis* and takes with him a young Indian boy named Namontack, who is to learn English and interpret. Namontack has been exchanged for young Thomas Savage who now lives in Werowocomoco, the village of paramount Chief Powhatan, and is to learn the Indian language and interpret.

Ten days later, on April 20, 1608, the rest of the First Supply, the ship the *Phoenix*, commanded by Captain Francis Nelson, arrives with 40 settlers and supplies. After being lost in the fog, Captain Nelson went to the West Indies to refit and take on fresh supplies.

The settlers now total 138 people, 60 and 40 from the two ships of the First Supply plus 38 who survive from the original adventurers.

SMITH MEETS 10 YEAR OLD POCAHONTAS

On June 2, 1608, John Smith writes a letter about Jamestown that is published in part, *A True Relation of*

Such Occurrences and Accidents of Note as Have Happened in Virginia Since the First Planting of That Colony Which Is Now Resident in the South Part Thereof, Till the Last Return. Smith tells of his December 1607 capture by the Indians and being taken to Chief Powhatan. He makes no mention of being attacked with clubs or of the presence of Pocahontas during his captivity. There is also no mention of being threatened with clubs and saved by Pocahontas in his 1612 book about his Virginia adventure.

In April 1608, Smith captures seven Paspaheghans Indians as a result of a trade disagreement. The Paspaheghans are one of about 31 tribes in the Powhatan confederacy. Smith first mentions Pocahontas in his June 1608 letter as part of Powhatan's response to his capture of the seven Paspaheghans in April 1608. Smith relates that in May 1608, Chief Powhatan sends a messenger Rawhunt, and his daughter, to secure the release of the Paspaheghans held by the colonists. He describes Pocahontas:

> Powhatan ... sent his daughter, a child of ten years old, which not only for feature, countenance, and proportion much exceedeth any of the rest of his people, but for wit and spirit the only nonpareil of his country. This he sent by his most trusty messenger, called Rawhunt ...

May 1608 is Pocahontas' first visit to the fort.

On September 10, 1608, John Smith is elected President of the Council of the Virginia colony. The colony is in trouble and has many minor gentry who refuse to do physical labor. He institutes a hard line stance of "He who does not work, will not eat." It is a necessary policy, but it makes him unpopular with many of the colonists.

SPANISH SETTLE SANTA FE, NEW MEXICO

Meanwhile, Santa Fe, New Mexico, is founded by the Spanish in 1608.

THE SECOND SUPPLY

Captain Christopher Newport and the Second Supply arrive in Jamestown on October 1, 1608, on the *Mary and Margaret*. He finds only 50 settlers alive of the 138 settlers alive a little over five months ago when the second ship of the First Supply arrived. Until Newport's arrival, 154 of a total of 204 settlers have died, or 75%.

Captain Newport brings 70 settlers, including two women, the first women to go to Virginia. The women are Mistress Forest, who comes with her husband Thomas Forest, and her maid Anne Burrows. With these additions, there are now 120 settlers.

JAMESTOWN'S FIRST WEDDING

Anne Burrows, who was one of the first two women to come to Jamestown as maid to Mistress Forest, marries John Layton, a carpenter. She bears four daughters and is still alive in 1624. That is remarkable longevity for the conditions she faced. She must have been a very strong person.

PLANS FOR THE THIRD SUPPLY

The Virginia Company of London knows they have to do something different to make the colony succeed. They decide to send a very large group of adventurers, 600 people, more than the total in three previous expeditions combined. John Rolfe joins the fleet of nine ships of the Third Supply and sails on the *Sea Venture* on May 15, 1609.

We have now arrived in the Historical Context at the beginning of our story.

DEDICATION AND ACKNOWLEDGMENTS

I dedicate this book to my wife Randy C. Rolfe, my children Jason John Rolfe and Tara C. Rolfe, my mother Virginia S. Rolfe who is now deceased, my father John Rolfe, my grandfather Harold John Rolfe, my great grandfather John Rolfe, and all the other John Rolfes who came before them.

I want to acknowledge and thank my wife Randy C. Rolfe for her encouragement and ceaseless support for this project. I am also very grateful for her tireless support of me personally, and of all my other projects.

I am grateful to my children Jason John Rolfe and Tara C. Rolfe for their support and encouragement.

I want to thank my father, John Rolfe, for teaching me the family history and for not acting too upset when I didn't always pay attention. If I had not learned the family tradition of naming the oldest male child John Rolfe, or some variation including John Rolfe, I may not have investigated my ancestor and discovered that John Rolfe was America's first entrepreneur. So thanks again, Dad.

I also want to thank my many friends who listened with often rapt attention as I told the amazing historical tale of John Rolfe's journey on the *Sea Venture* and how he survived the wreck of the *Sea Venture*, how he saved the Virginia colony by developing a successful cash crop for export, how he saved the colony by bringing about the Peace of Pocahontas through his marriage, how that peace allowed the colony to grow strong enough to resist expulsion by the Indians, how he was responsible for our young nation being and speaking English rather than French, Spanish, or Dutch, and how he participated in the first ever representative body in the new world which led to the unique American form of government. John Rolfe's marriage to Pocahontas was also significant as the first interracial church marriage in the Americas. I was, and still remain, very excited by John Rolfe's story and his impact on the founding of America and on American entrepreneurship, so thanks to my friends for listening.

    I am grateful to Don Cochran who provided valuable research material, and to those who read the manuscript and gave valuable feedback, including Albert Mazzone, Skip Chalfant, Lee Stivale, John David Rolfe (no close relation to me that I know of), and Randy Rolfe. The final book is much improved for their comments.

OTHER BOOKS BY JOHN L. ROLFE

PRINCESS BUTTERCUP THE CAT'S CROSS-COUNTRY ROAD TRIP #3, co-author with Princess Buttercup The Cat and Randy C. Rolfe. Princess Buttercup The Cat can't type and can't even hold a pen – no opposable thumb – so John L. Rolfe followed her directions and typed the manuscript and prepared it for publication.

THE AFFIRMATIONS BOOK FOR SHARING, co-author with Randy C. Rolfe.

ABOUT THE AUTHOR

JOHN L. ROLFE

John L. Rolfe is a retired Philadelphia lawyer who has represented hundreds of entrepreneurs, helping them establish and grow their businesses and their profitability. He earned his Bachelor degree in Marketing from the Wharton School of the University of Pennsylvania, and his Juris Doctor degree from the University of Pennsylvania Law School. He also earned a Master of Laws degree in Tax Law from Temple University School of Law.

As an entrepreneur, Rolfe has developed a successful real estate investment business. He also markets his own large colorful paintings. In addition, he has co-authored two previous books, one with his wife and one with his cat. He also developed the marketing plan for his wife's first book, which propelled her to fame and dozens of TV talk show appearances as a parenting author.

John L. Rolfe always knew John Rolfe was an ancestor, but it was only after investigating the history of entrepreneurship that he realized that John Rolfe started it all in America. He was America's First Entrepreneur. John L. Rolfe's passion is sharing what he has learned with groups large and small.

He is the father of two grown children and lives with his first and only wife and their cat Princess Buttercup The Cat. They divide their time between their homes in Pennsylvania and California. Rolfe enjoys reading, movies, classic and exotic cars, wine, Belgian ales, food, and travel.

John L. Rolfe is available for corporate speaking and consulting. For more information, please go to www.JohnLRolfe.com.

For more information on the historical subject matter of *America's First Entrepreneur*, please go to www.AmericasFirstEntrepreneur.com.

CPSIA information can be obtained
at www.ICGtesting.com
Printed in the USA
LVOW04s1621230516

489544LV00052B/1690/P

9 781467 950817